Hannah Perkins Dodge, William Jacob Cloues

A Teacher's Message

A Memorial of Hannah Perkins Dodge

Hannah Perkins Dodge, William Jacob Cloues

A Teacher's Message
A Memorial of Hannah Perkins Dodge

ISBN/EAN: 9783337812768

Printed in Europe, USA, Canada, Australia, Japan

Cover: Foto ©Thomas Meinert / pixelio.de

More available books at **www.hansebooks.com**

A TEACHER'S MESSAGE

A Memorial of

HANNAH PERKINS DODGE.

1821–1896.

Prepared by

WILLIAM J. CLOUES.

BOSTON:
1896.

COPYRIGHT, 1896.

BY WILLIAM J. CLOUES.

Press of
ALFRED MUDGE & SON.
Boston.

IN MEMORY OF HER

WHOSE FRIENDSHIP WAS A PRIVILEGE AND TREASURE

This Volume

IS GRATEFULLY DEDICATED TO HER

BROTHERS AND SISTER.

My immortal mind is a casket more valuable than gems of earth or sea. My earnest endeavors shall henceforth be directed to the storing of it with jewels worthy of a place therein.

H. P. DODGE.

Essay, Oct. 30, 1844.

CONTENTS.

	PAGE.
ADDRESS	7
TRIBUTES	30
MEMORIAL ADDRESS	37
SELECTIONS IN POETRY:	
Oh! I would live in visions!	49
All things speak to me	50
All things smile	51
Nature	52
The Ideal in Nature	53
Smiles of Eden	53
On a Spring-like Day in Mid-winter	55
Song of the Indian Summer Spirits	55
The Lover's Jubilate	56
The Organ	57
Recantation	58
To a Star	59
Thoughts at Eventide	60
From my Heart,—a Mood	60
The Ride	62
What is Man?	63
The Pauper's Funeral	64
Morning Hymn	65
Evening Hymn	65
Song	66
The Hours	67
North School Song	68

CONTENTS.

The Erl King	69
My Gold and my Jewels	71
The Ideal	72

SELECTIONS IN PROSE:

Talks to her Pupils.

I.	Self-government	75
II.	Industry	86
III.	Wisdom	93
IV.	Friendship and Love	100
V.	The Study of Nature	108
VI.	Womanly Virtue	113

BENEVOLENCE	122
ART EDUCATION	126
ENGRAVING	145
CATHEDRALS	153
MICHAEL ANGELO	157
WINDS AND WAVES	166
THE TEACHER AND HER WORK	168
LETTERS OF TRAVEL	175
MISCELLANEOUS SELECTIONS	182
SONNET	201

A TEACHER'S MESSAGE.

HANNAH PERKINS DODGE.

1821-1896.

MISS DODGE died on the morning of Jan. 11, 1896, at her residence in Littleton, Mass., at the age of seventy-four years, eleven months. The funeral services, attended by many relatives and friends, were held in the Baptist meetinghouse, Littleton, Mass., Jan. 15, 1896. They were conducted by her pastor, Rev. William J. Clones, and included Scripture readings: the hymns, "O God, our help in ages past," "A mighty fortress is our God," and "Beneath the cross of Jesus"; prayer by Rev. R. G. Johnson, of West Medway; an address on her life and character by the pastor; and the reading of extracts from letters received from the following friends and eminent persons by whom she was well beloved: Rev. C. H. Spalding, Mrs. D. H. Rice, Prof. L. E. Warren, Rev. A. N. Dary, Miss S. F. White, Miss H. S. Mead, Rev. G. W. Gile, Rev. W. H. Eaton, Dr. H. L. Wayland, Dr. Edward G. Porter, and Dr. Edward Everett Hale. She was laid to rest in the cemetery in Littleton.

AN ADDRESS

DELIVERED JAN. 15, 1896, BY THE REV.
WILLIAM J. CLOUES, ON THE LIFE
AND CHARACTER OF MISS
HANNAH P. DODGE.

THE town of Littleton to-day mourns the loss of one of the most talented, distinguished, and revered daughters in its history. While, in the decease of Miss Hannah P. Dodge, the church universal, as well as our own church, loses one whose rare gifts and noble ministrations were always consecrated to God's service, the cause of higher education also is deprived of one of its noblest endowed and most successful teachers of young women. From to-day on, as the sad news finds its way to former associates and more remote pupils in all parts of our land, there will be sorrow at the great loss sustained. Yet our common sorrow can dull but little the keen sense of our personal bereavement. The sentence of

Goethe's, one of her favorite quotations, "All is fruit, and all is seed," finds remarkable fulfilment in the rich fruitage of her own life and character, and in the high aspirations she awakened in other lives.

Miss Dodge was born at the old homestead in North Littleton, Feb. 16, 1821. Very early in life there were indications to parents and friends that she had been endowed naturally with gifts of no ordinary kind. She was brought up as a farmer's daughter, and inherited from her honored parents, Barnabas and Sarah Dodge, and from her ancestors,— at least three of whom served in the War of the Revolution, one of them being a captain in Col. Gerrish's regiment in service at the Battle of Bunker Hill, — certain sturdy and admirable traits of character. These, in her case, found expression in an early and absorbing thirst for knowledge and a desire for a broad and thorough education. From her father she received that love of books which led him to establish two small village libraries, and which, in order to arouse a similar interest among his children, caused him to spend the long winter evenings in reading aloud to them from book or paper as they gathered around the cheerful hearth. From her mother she received that capacity for administration which commanded the admiration of so many and contributed no small part to her success. At the district school she gave frequent evidence of the possession of that vigorous and fertile mind destined to do so much for her pupils. In an early composition she aptly likened her mind to a golden and jewelled casket placed in her hands for use and blessing. When only twelve years old, on March 19, 1833, she obtained one of the small but much coveted prizes offered by the Littleton Lyceum for excellence in English composition. While it was also early realized that she possessed high moral qualities, —

> "The full, rich nature, free to trust,
> Truthful and almost sternly just,
> Impulsive, earnest, prompt to act,
> And make her generous thought a fact,
> Keeping with many a light disguise
> The secret of self-sacrifice."

When seventeen years of age she taught her first school, receiving for her services but one dollar a week and her board. This school was the one situated in Groton, between Forge Village and the old Ridge Tavern. This marked the beginning of her long and successful career as an educator. For several terms, the last ending April 5, 1843, she taught the old North School of Littleton, in whose famous reunions she, and her younger and lamented sister Emma, took so lively an interest, and where, years later, her sister, Miss Nancy P. Dodge, also taught.

This was succeeded by several terms of teaching in the two earlier schools in the Nashoba district: Miss Dodge being the second woman to teach a Littleton district school in the important winter term.

In these first years of teaching she was accustomed to visit the schools of neighboring teachers in Littleton and elsewhere, and to attend school institutes, in order to improve her own methods of instruction and discipline. And many tributes given then and since, by these first pupils, show how she won their love and esteem as well as their honor and respect.

On July 5, 1840, she was baptized by the Rev. Oliver Ayer into the membership of this church. During the more than half a century since that time, she has loyally retained her membership with us, and thereby imparted to the home church the lustre of her fame and character.

During the time from March, 1840, until March, 1841, she was a student for several months in Lawrence Academy, Groton. From there she went to the Townsend Female Seminary, an institution of learning then among the first of its class in the land. It was at that time thriving under the efficient direction of the late Miss Ruth S. Robinson, a woman of rare judgment and mental attainment, the sister of the revered Ezekiel G. Robinson, once president of Brown University. Here Miss Dodge's varied talents found wider fields for their development. And in her bright young face, that

> "Countenance in which did meet
> Sweet records, promises as sweet."

her teachers also saw

> "The reason firm, the temperate will,
> Endurance, foresight, strength, and skill;
> A perfect woman, nobly planned,
> To warn, to comfort, and command.
> And yet a spirit still, and bright
> With something of an angel light."

Soon after her graduation, in 1843, she was recalled to her Alma Mater to take her place among its teachers. Then after only one year's service was called in 1846, at the age of twenty-five years, to occupy the important position of Principal, a place at that time of marked distinction. For seven years, with widening success, she filled this position. In addition to her duties as Principal, she taught Latin, Mental and Moral Philosophy, Drawing, and Painting. Her remarkable resources for these duties became increasingly apparent. Scores of pupils, many of them living to-day, could testify to the great intellectual and spiritual quickening imparted to them in the class-rooms and dormitories at Townsend. Here was awakened in other hearts a love like her own for the beautiful in art and nature, literature and life. Here, through her poetical gifts, lofty and choice thought found form and substance in several beautiful poems: her spirit of devotion moving her to write several morning and evening hymns for use in the public exercises. In the early part of 1852 she visited Norfolk, Va., and taught several months in the school of Miss Ruth Robinson. In the fall and winter of 1852-53 she attended sessions of the Normal School, Boston, and presumably taught classes there.

In November, 1853, she felt obliged, on account of ill health, to resign her position at Townsend. But her rest was not a long one. She was next called, September, 1854, to be Principal of the Oread Institute for Young Ladies at Worcester, where her former success as a teacher and Principal was continued and established. Here, on one of Worcester's beautiful hills, in the buildings which architecturally reminded the passing stranger of some castle overlooking the Rhine, Miss Dodge gathered about her scores of young women. To them she became the embodiment of all that was inspiring and elevating in education, art, and morals. The English department, including Mathematics, Rhetoric, Natural Sciences, Mental and Moral Philosophy, was under her personal supervision, with the well-beloved Elizabeth Arms Wayland, formerly associated with her at Townsend, as her assistant: the department of ancient and modern languages being under the direction of Professor H. W. Carstens.

Here Miss Dodge employed her moments of relaxation from school duties in rendering into English poetry some of the classic poems of Goethe and Schiller. Her class-room work, always of a high order, was daily supplemented by the influence of her gracious and strong personality, while she sought to impart to her school, as far as possible, the atmosphere of home. In this larger educational centre she formed life-long friendships with prominent and well-known educators and philanthropists. Among her advisers were President Francis Wayland of Brown, his son, Dr. H. L. Wayland, then pastor of the Main Street Baptist Church, Worcester, now of Philadelphia, Dr. E. E. Hale, Hon. Eli Thayer, Hon. Isaac Davis, H. S. Washburn, Esq., Dr. Barnas Sears, and others.

In all her work at Worcester, as always elsewhere, she failed not, in the faithful devotion to her calling, to invariably give due recognition to the religious instincts of her pupils, both in public exercises and in class-room work. She planned to educate her pupils in righteousness and holiness, as well as in mental alertness and literary and linguistic skill.

In the summer of 1859 she laid aside her school cares for a year of travel and study in Europe. During this time, in company with Mrs. Caroline W. Horton, she visited, Paris, Cologne, the Rhine, Heidelberg, Lucerne, Geneva, Milan, Florence, Pompeii, Rome, Genoa, Venice, Dresden, London, Edinburgh, and many other famous places. She studied the modern languages, French, German, and Italian, in their homes, and still further developed her talent for art under skilful Italian and German teachers in Rome and Dresden. Returning to her own country in the summer of 1860, better prepared than ever before for her chosen work by her extended observation, studies, and experience, thoroughly familiar with the best methods of instruction abroad, Miss Dodge opened, Oct. 22, 1861, her remarkably successful school for young ladies at Codman Hill, Milton, Dorchester. She stated her high aim in the following language of her first circular :

" It is the aim of the Principal, not only to furnish every facility for intellectual development, but to surround the pupil by those influences which will elevate and develop the character. All mental progress must be subservient to this end; to the attainment of which, high culture is of inestimable value. The accomplishments are not of necessity showy appendages to a superficial education: but, in connection with a well-disciplined mind, are themselves a means of developing the powers, cultivating the taste, and beautifying the whole character. We would send forth educated American, Christian women, who may illustrate the noble part woman is capable of acting in the advanced civilization of the age."

With experienced teachers to assist her, among whom were Miss M. S. Clapp, Mr. Charles Ansorge, Madame Doudiet, Prof. Hermann Daum, and Miss Sarah F. White, during all the uncertain years of the war, Miss Dodge made the Codman Hill School so desirable an educational shrine, that to it many of the choicest and brightest young women from the best homes of New England and elsewhere found their way. This school, her own creation, may be accounted, for many reasons, her most successful venture as an educator and administrator. It was started and carried on amidst difficulties and under limitations which would have proven fatal to the plans of a less resolute and experienced educator. But she, whose ambition from early years had been to live, to learn, to grow, persevered, and saw many of her choicest hopes realized in the successes of the Codman Hill school.

After completing her work at Codman Hill, in 1866, Miss Dodge spent several months in rest and recuperation. From September, 1868, to June, 1870, she successfully filled the office of Lady Principal of the Ladies' Collegiate Department, of Kalamazoo College, Michigan. She then returned to New England again. In September, 1872, she became a member of the faculty of the New London Literary and Scientific Institution, now Colby Academy, New London, N. H., of which Prof. Laban E. Warren, now of Waterville, Me., was then president. In September, 1874, she was called to assume the responsible position of Lady Principal, succeeding Miss Mary O. Carter. This same position she had been asked to occupy, the first one to receive the invitation, over twenty years before. She filled this office until June, 1877, during one of the most critical periods in the history of that institution. Her services to it and to the cause of education, at a time when burdens were many and heavy, were of great value, especially since she brought to the task her wide experience and skill as a teacher, her rare natural gifts, and her influence from previous successes. She taught the most advanced classes in the school. Her department included German, English Literature, Political Economy, Mental and Moral Philosophy, and the Evidences of Christianity.

In 1877 she resigned her position, and then, after spending some forty years in faithful services as an educator, she came back to her native town for the rest so laboriously earned. But the cause of education still called her, and, as so often before, the call met from her a generous response. During four successive years, 1878–1882, the people and schools of Littleton were privileged to enjoy her valuable services as the only Lady Superintendent of schools it has ever had. In 1879 she prepared and read her valuable historical address in the observance of the semi-centennial of our Lyceum. For various occasions having prepared and given lectures on "Churches and Cathedrals," "The Chrysalis," on "Winds and Waves," and on "Thought expressed by Art," many made known to her their desire to hear her in the Lyceum course. Accordingly, in 1881, she complied with the wishes of her friends and gave an interesting and successful lecture on one of her favorite artists, "Michael Angelo." Heartily interested in the establishment of the Reuben Hoar Library, she was elected a member of the Board of Trustees, and served as its secretary from its organization in 1885 to March, 1893. To her efforts, as a member of the Soliciting Committee for raising the library subscription fund, she herself heading the list with a generous amount, and writing able articles for the press in advocacy of the plan, is due in a measure our possession of such a beneficial institution. In March and April, 1886, in company with her friend, the late Mrs. Lucy M. Kimball, she joined a party of excursionists and visited Mexico; this journey being one of several which Miss Dodge undertook from time to time to enlarge her knowledge of her own land and its people, or to visit her friends in their homes. An active worker in the temperance cause, for several years she was the first president of the local Women's Christian Temperance Union, and at the convention held here in 1890 gave the address of welcome for the society. Thus her influence was felt in all the homes of Littleton. It is certainly no easy task to speak of her services in our church. These have been many, varied, and unceasing. In every part of our church life her influence has been felt.

"The blessing of her quiet life
   Fell on us like the dew.
And good thoughts, where her footsteps pressed,
   Like fairy blossoms grew.

"Sweet promptings unto kindest deeds
   Were in her very look.
We read her face, as one who reads
   A true and holy book."

She was for many years the beloved president of our Ladies' Circle, and teacher of a large class in our Sunday school. And served, as only she could, as a member of many committees, appointed for various purposes. It is due largely to her efforts and aid that we enjoy the possession of many things which contribute to the efficiency and success of the work of our church.

How many have known of her kindnesses, her benevolences, her philanthropies, especially in mission fields. How widely, how judiciously, how unobtrusively, she gave; if not always in a financial way, yet, after all, perhaps in a more valuable way, in kindly advice and sympathetic counsel. She wanted to share her possessions with others, as they can testify who remember her Shakespearian Club; her lectures on Art, Engravings, and Pictures in the "Pastor's Literary Hours" several years ago; her interest in our young men's reading-room in our vestry one winter, and her support of it; her familiar basket of photographs and curiosities for the table at the church social, her beautiful and interesting readings at the same; her many gifts fashioned by her own hands for little ones among her friends; her genial sharing with her guests the painting, the book, the flower which had brought light and joy to her own life; her delightful letters of consolation and counsel upon the most varied topics and in reply to a great variety of requests; her sprightly narration of some anecdote or incident or reminiscence which she had found in her reading; and last of all, the unfolding, as of some rare exotic, of her rich and manifold spiritual experiences to her pastor and her nearest friends.

In the delineation of her character I feel she would say,

"Banish all compliments but single truth."

And yet, any attempt to tell what she was, so rare was her nature as a whole, and so unusual her successes, might indeed seem, to one who did not know her, friendship's exaggeration. But, when you consider what it meant fifty years ago for a young woman to start out, as she did, from a secluded farmer's home, with bright face, eager step, and ambitious spirit, to make something of herself in the world, and to be of service to others in one of God's noblest and most exacting vocations: and when you hear, though in how meagre a way, to what she attained, you cannot fail to realize, that she indeed possessed great gifts of mind and heart, harmonized into beautiful and attractive symmetry of character.

Miss Dodge combined qualities not often found in the same person. She had a nature responsive, almost to pain, to the beautiful, the true, the good in everything: to which her paintings, poems, and teachings, her conversation, and home surroundings, all bore witness. But she was also very practical in matters of daily life, precise in manners, accurate in language, keen in business, wise in finance. The motto she once gave her pupils was true of herself. She planned for eternity and lived by the day.

Miss Dodge possessed a keen intellect, stored with choice knowledge and wisdom, sharpened by years of study and discipline in the works of Bishop Butler, Paley, Hopkins, Wayland, and others: so that, until the infirmity of advancing age hindered, it was always ready to inquire, to investigate, to analyze the subject in hand, whatever it might be. She was a born reasoner. She could state her own opinions clearly, strongly, tersely. She could give a reason for her conclusion. She seldom trusted her intuitions alone. In this her mind had that grasp and vigor which is now no longer attributed exclusively to man. Then, on the other hand, she could enter with rare appreciation into the realms of the unseen, the visionary, the fanciful, with the poets of the ages for her companions, particularly with her favorite authors, Shakespeare, Dante, Goethe, Emerson, Browning, and Tennyson. The poet and financier rarely dwell in the same mind. The philosopher and artist are not usually thus associated in the same person.

She was one whose friendship was a choice treasure. She was a welcome guest as the cherished friend of many homes. While always glad to commend a friend's best effort, she never harshly criticised a physical defect or an unavoidable mistake. Her championship of her friends was always decided, strong, certain. Do the best you possibly can, — this had been her life-long aim. She asked that of those about her; more than that she never demanded. Her friendship was perhaps best illustrated in the affection, service, and fidelity of her attendants and companions during many years, one of whom* had preceded her into the unseen world by only a few months, as if, it would seem, to be present to welcome her dear and revered earthly friend to the home of heavenly light as she had so often welcomed her here.

Miss Dodge's religious experience grew in richness and beauty with her mental growth. She was always an appreciative listener and devout worshipper, constant in her attendance, even after her bodily infirmity rendered it less enjoyable to her. She loved the Scriptures and welcomed the best and freshest thought on Biblical doctrines. She could and did sift the chaff from the wheat. She did not as often as others speak of her experience; sometimes, in her quiet and touching way, said she had none. But all the time her heart was glowing with love to her Christ and her God, and her mind planning some new way of serving him by serving those about her. She was thoroughly genuine and real in her religious life. She abhorred all cant and sham and hypocrisy. To her mind, the

---

* Miss Hannah M. Neagle, died Sept. 27, 1895, at the age of 29 years.

religion of Christ never needed apology. A religious profession might. The common-sense view of religion that it was not intended to make our joys less, nor to take from our enjoyment of all that is true and beautiful in God's world, found a ready advocate in her. When of late years she talked with me of the unseen into which she was one day to enter, while her mind was perplexed over its mysteries, there was always the repose of spirit upon the Christian's hope and the Christian's heaven.

What a cherished and unfading picture in the memories of all those who were ever privileged to enter its portals was that home which our dear friend made so attractive and beautiful. How eager was her desire to please in the entertainment of her guest, whether a stranger or friend. It was worth many a day's journey to be welcomed in that dignified and queenly manner so familiar to her friends, to sit in her presence and look into that silvery-crowned face from which the light of its "eternal summer shall never fade" from many lives, to listen to that conversation in which philosophy and the common-place, travel and art, poetry and reminiscence, wit and reason, science and religion, were so wonderfully blended, to have the attention turned to the fragrant blossom, the beautiful picture or the tinted sky, and after it all to be speeded on your way with the impression somehow formed, you knew not how, that she and not yourself was the favored one by your visit. And thus we shall think of her, and not as in the silence of death, until by and by we shall hope to meet again that beautiful soul which could make even the earthly features seem sometimes to shine with an almost heavenly radiance.

And if our loss be great and so keenly felt, what must it be to the bereaved family, to whom this life came so near. They indeed may feel assured that many prayers ascend for them, and sincere sympathies from many hearts are shared with them in this sad separation.

May our Heavenly Father in his merciful love comfort us, bear us up, grant unto us his shepherding care through all our life, and bestow upon us, in his Son Jesus Christ our Lord, those consolations and hopes which often comforted our departed friend, and which shall bring us at last, one by one, into the light and peace and joy of eternal life and reunion in the heavenly mansions; and may the memories, few or many, of all that Hannah Perkins Dodge was in her life and character never be blotted out of our minds, but remain from this day on to serve as a constant inspiration for all that is pure and elevating, beautiful, charitable and womanly, in Christian character. Many years ago Miss Dodge wrote the following poem, entitled, "Mors mea ne careat lacrymis," which may appropriately conclude this address: —

  Oh, who will weep when I am gone,
    Who will for me the fond tear shed?
  Will there be those who loved me well,
    To weep beside my dying bed?

  Among the crowd that greet me now
    With kindly smile or friendly word,
  Oh, is there one my form will miss,
    One heart with grief for me be stirred?

  I would not seek the dark, cold grave,
    With no one left to weep for me,
  I would not break all ties of earth,
    And my last gaze no tear-drop see!

  E'en Christian faith is not yet sight,
    Though Heaven my home, the grave's its way;
  And who would plunge in Death's cold flood,
    With no loved voice to bid him stay?

Oh, dreary is the path I tread,
    Bittered my cup of life with woe;
Oh, sad no hearts to mine so grown,
    That rent apart no tear will flow!

I would the flow'rs my hand should strew
    The plants of healing I should spread,
Should thrive in blessed and faithful hearts,
    And drop their dews when I am dead.

Grief for the loved no canker leaves,
    The mourning house robs not its guests,
The softening tears from sorrow's fount
    Are blessings to our human breasts.

The Man of Sorrows wept to see
    The ravages of sin and death,
Wept when he saw the loved one's form
    With pulses stilled, and silent breath.

I would not those I leave behind
    Should be by bread of sorrow fed,
But oh! I would not, cannot die,
    And think no one a tear will shed!

"Blessed are the dead which die in the Lord from henceforth: Yea, saith the Spirit, that they may rest from their labors; and their works do follow them." Amen.

TRIBUTES.

"I have never known a more helpful friend, or a fuller life, and it has been my privilege to be intimately acquainted with her from my childhood. She was reticent in regard to her spiritual life, but she loved goodness wherever she found it, and she never allowed difference of opinion to influence her friendships." — Miss HANNAH S. MEAD, *Jamaica Plain, Mass.*

"It is many years since I have had the pleasure of meeting Miss Dodge; but whenever I saw her I learned something which was of value in the great interests of education. I know what a loss she must be, not simply to the members of her own family, but to the community." — EDWARD EVERETT HALE, *Roxbury, Mass.*

"It is a great pleasure to have my memory enriched, not only by her later friendship, but by the unique image of that bright young life starting out from its somewhat isolated surroundings, and rapidly winning way to places of eminence. . . . Her ideal for those under her charge was as lofty as she held it for her own inspiration, nor was it ever lowered for the comfort of the lazy or in deference to mediocrity. Press on, press on, always seemed to be her motto." — Miss SARAH F. WHITE, *Littleton, Mass.*

"Miss Dodge had fine graces of character. To a pure and beautiful life she most happily united modesty of manner, gentleness of spirit, and earnestness of high purpose. Her beautiful life has ended in peace. Her home of culture and art recalls such noble women as Celia Thaxter and Lucy Larcom. She has left the savor of a sweet life of Christian trust. She wore in life the humble yet exalted character of a saint of God, and more and more will that character attach to her sacred and precious memory. She was true to the sincere faith of her early years. She was genuinely catholic and as genuinely conservative. Her life is a strong testimony to the value of religion, a testimony she has sealed with her death." — Rev. C. H. SPALDING, *Cambridge, Mass.*

"Miss Dodge was a teacher of uncommon powers. Her very presence was a benediction to her pupils. She combined gracefulness with authority in such a degree that all in the classroom felt restrained from all that savored of disorder, and yet inspired with a sense of ease and self-possession. She was a thorough scholar, with a happy faculty of imparting what she knew. Her words were like apples of gold in pictures of silver. She impressed her own thoughts and spirit upon the lives of her scholars in a remarkable manner. She taught them to think and reason for themselves and not to lean wholly upon their text book. She had a high ideal of what it was to be a true scholar, and incorporated this idea in the minds of those who sought her instruction. And above all, she taught by precept and example that all knowledge and all accomplishments should be for Christ and not for self." — Rev. WM. H. EATON, *Nashua, N. H.*

"Miss Dodge was a noble woman. She was loved and honored here in Colby Academy. She was held in warm esteem by all who knew her. The world is poorer and heaven is richer in the death of this Christian woman." — Rev. GEO. W. GILE, *President of Colby Academy, New London, N.H.*

"Miss Dodge's name has long been familiar in our family. From the day when she established her famous school for girls at Codman Hill — quite near us — we have known and honored and loved her. . . . Her influence over her pupils was greatly increased by her personal force of character, which, adorned as it was by culture, was particularly strong in its moral qualities. There was always a reserve of pure, spiritual enlightenment in the woman, a pleasing combination of grace and strength, which made her not only the head of the school, but the personal guide and counsellor of her girls, who all felt that she stood to them in the place of a mother, tried and true. Let us hope that the town and the Commonwealth will long continue to produce such worthy types of womanhood as we have known and esteemed in our departed friend." — EDWARD G. PORTER, D. D., *Ashmont, Mass.*

"Miss Dodge was an intimate and valued friend of myself and my family for more than forty years. I have very highly prized her character and admired her career. From the first she aimed to rise and to attain eminence and usefulness in her profession. Beginning to teach in a district school when little more than a girl, she availed herself of every opportunity for enlarging her knowledge and elevating her standards. . . . Naturally she rose in her profession; and every advancement in position and opportunity was made the means of still further advancement in attainment and qualification. She had, in an eminent degree, professional and intellectual conscientiousness; she withheld nothing of study or labor by which she might make her instructions of greater value. Her intellectual sympathies were broad; she embraced in the line of her thought and study, history, art, ethics, language, literature. Her high sense of the dignity of the teacher's profession, and her conscientious desire to fulfil to the utmost its demands, and to leave nothing undone that might add to the richness of her stores, and to her equipment in the art of imparting, characterized her in youth and in middle age, and I doubt not up to the close of her years as a teacher. I also honored the public spirit which led her to accept the duties of superintendent of schools, and to discharge these duties with such conscientious fidelity. I cannot doubt that her eminently useful career was a part of the debt which Massachusetts owes to Horace Mann. Her aroused interest and ambition were no doubt a part of the result of the educational revival of which he was so largely the means. She everywhere achieved success and usefulness as a teacher, and was an honor to the calling to which her entire life was devoted.

Her life as a whole exhibits an eminent example of what may be obtained by a New England girl, who, with no extraordinary educational advantages, sets herself to making the most of herself and of her opportunities. I consider it a great honor that I and my family were numbered among her friends. She closes a life devoted to the welfare of her fellow beings, and especially of the young, and has gone to receive the reward of those who rest from their labors, and their works follow them." — H. L. WAYLAND, D. D., *Philadelphia.*

SELECTIONS

FROM THE

WRITINGS

OF

HANNAH PERKINS DODGE.

On the seventy-fifth anniversary of the birth of Miss Dodge, Feb. 16, 1896, a commemorative service was held in the Baptist meeting house, Littleton, Mass. At this service, in which all the Littleton churches united, Rev. L. B. Voorhees, of Groton, read the scriptures, and Rev. I. F. Porter offered prayer. Rev. William J. Cloues gave the address which follows, and then occupied the rest of the time allotted for the service in reading selections in prose and poetry from the writings of Miss Dodge. These selections were gathered from her literary possessions, of which the greater part were left in manuscript. A large number of friends and relatives attended the service, to whom it was of the deepest interest and profit. The present volume was suggested during the preparation for this memorial meeting.

A TEACHER'S MESSAGE.

ADDRESS BY THE REV. WILLIAM J. CLOUES.

"She openeth her mouth with wisdom; and in her tongue is the law of kindness." — Prov. xxxi. 26.

Some lives are inspirations. They shine as stars. Their influence never wanes, but increases with years. In their light we live to the accomplishment of noble actions. Their counsels while among the living, their works when they are dead, guide us over many perilous pathways to high achievements ourselves. And it sometimes happens that however many and great their works during their lifetime, they are even more valued for what they accomplish afterwards in the hearts of those influenced by them. One such life we commemorate to-night. Seventy-five years ago to-day, Feb. 16, 1821, it began its bright and beautiful career. Some of you have been privileged to watch its growth upward, outward, onward, during all these years. You have known of its quiet beginnings, its eager outreachings after wisdom and truth. You have seen the things dreamed of in maidenhood's thoughtful hour actually come to pass. You have seen it go from one success to another in its noble and glorious calling. This one would be a teacher, — a teacher, fully equipped, richly endowed, widely influential: a Christian teacher of young women. True to this aim it went on, until in course of time, scores and hundreds of bright young pupils looked to Miss Hannah P. Dodge as one of the mightiest influences for the good, the true, the beautiful, wherever found, which ever entered their lives.

And, as autumn grain under the farmer's skilful toil, it multiplied over and over again its usefulness and richness. The heights attained in maturity were as prophetic fulfilments of early resolutions and promises. The hope of becoming was changed to the blessing of being. Faithful cultivation of mind and heart under her Divine Master's tuition bore at last that fine fruit of Christian character so well known to us all. Rare indeed it is to find a life so symmetrically fashioned. What development of many talents; what discipline of all its powers; what gradual expansion of reason and imagination, taste and sensibility, judgment and conscience! Do you wonder her pupils and friends thus wrote to her? "If my life is a success, it will be due to you." "You will always be young to me. I cannot think of you as growing old." "How thankful I am for the many lessons and words of counsel you have given me." "How grand your mission passed in supplying parents' deficiencies and correcting their errors." "A conversation with you was like a tonic." "You were as a well-spring of mental inspiration to me." "How prized were your strong and spiritual talks to your pupils."

And yet all this attainment and helpfulness came through much toil, pain, and self-denial. In 1842, at the end of her first three weeks at Townsend as a scholar, she wrote to a friend, "My studies occupy almost all my time, and ought to my whole. I am so dull and stupid that I am obliged to study pretty hard, and as you are well aware that I have no genius to aid me, you will not be surprised."

The effort and pains she took to grow in Christian grace and to possess a strong and useful character, is seen in these early resolutions: —

"May 2, 1841. *Resolved.* That I will be more conscientious in the performance of duty; that I will endeavor to give no one occasion to speak ill of me, or of religion on my account."

"Oct. 24, 1841. *Resolved.* That I will not ascribe unworthy motives for conduct of which I know nothing; that I will endeavor not even to think evil of others; that I will pray against this easily besetting sin."

In the summer of 1843 this purpose is jotted down: "I will endeavor to improve every moment in the acquisition of knowledge or otherwise improving myself."

And on the Sabbath, Jan. 16, 1848, while Principal of Townsend Seminary, she wrote this meditation: —

"The best and indeed the only way for me to succeed in my labors in the seminary here is to give myself wholly to my work without thought of emoluments or what will be said or thought of my course. I must forget myself, my own reputation or my own labors, and labor constantly, humbly, thoroughly, in whatever my hands find to do. If I do well, my reward of success is sure; if ill, no exertion of mine to keep up appearance of well-doing will succeed. I feel sure that I shall meet with all the success in my labors as a teacher that I deserve. Oh, that I may ever be found walking humbly and prayerfully before God, and be able fully to forget myself in my duties!"

As early as 1834 she began to draw and paint, and in 1836 to attempt English Composition as a mode for the expression of her thoughts. Even in these crude yet interesting productions there is some indication of those talents which, after only twelve years have elapsed, are to place her at the head of the Townsend Female Seminary.

In one of her first composition books there are attempts at composition on such subjects as "The Joys and Sorrows of the Teacher," "Things to be Avoided in Manners," "The Fountain by the Roadside," "There is Beauty Everywhere," "The Influence of Education upon the Countenance." I will venture to quote, in passing, a few sentences from some of these first attempts in which there is much that is interesting.

In one entitled "On the Comparative

Value of Novels and Biography," she appears as the defender of novels, contending that they furnish pleasure and relaxation, and form a good taste for writing or speaking. And thus concludes this early piece of writing: "I am not a professed novel reader, and on this ground I hope that some of my faults in writing will be pardoned."

In the same year, 1836, there is a short essay on the Indian, in which this occurs: "'If lion could paint,' said this monarch of the forest, 'instead of pictures of men killing lions, you would see those of lions killing men.' So with the Indian: if they could write, instead of stories of Indians killing white men, we might read those of white men killing Indians." From another essay of the same date, written fifty years ago, I cull these two sentences: "The teacher should be superior to the scholar, to teach him with advantage." "If one person is well educated, it does not make another less so."

These compositions, increasing in interest and successfulness, were upon many subjects: "Early Rising," "Can Gold gain Friendship?" "The Price of a Lasting

Fame," "The Mind is the Standard of the Man," "The Death of Cain," "Schools," "Five Minutes too Late," "The Mind capable of Infinite Progression," "The Triumphs of Truth," "The Scriptures of God," "History," "Progress of Education," "Learning for its own Sake."

"The spirit walks of every day deceased,
And smiles an angel, or a fury frowns."

"Nil mortalibus arduum est."

From the time Miss Dodge became Principal of Townsend Seminary, until within a few years of her death, she continued to develop her skill and talent in writing. Some of these literary attempts, especially in poetry, were for her own eye alone; others for a variety of occasions. She wrote poems, hymns, colloquies (on the avocations of women and favorite historical women), addresses to her pupils, translations in verse, lectures, letters of travel, humorous sketches, brief essays on many subjects for the Lesbian Society and the Reading Circle, for the *Oreadum*, the *Revolving Light*, the *Colby Voice*, the *Watchman*, the *National Baptist*, and other papers. But whatever the nature of the literary work in hand, Miss Dodge regarded it as secondary to her work as a teacher. The principal aim of her life was to teach, not to write. But while this aim in no way detracted from the power of her reasoning, the strength of her thought or the vigor of her imagination, it must, however, be kept in mind that she did not herself claim for any of her productions unusual literary merit. Still, she never ceased to regard all of them with peculiar interest as being the genuine expression of the changing moods of her spirit, and some of them as the utterance of her highest thought and a part of her best life.

Her choice of word and phrase, the loftiness of her thought and beauty of her style, the variety and suggestiveness of her writings, render them of more than ordinary value to young people. They are a precious heirloom to her friends, and will make many new friends among those who come to a knowledge of them; for they reprove listlessness and inactivity, awake to thoughtfulness and investigation, and by their swift and piercing spiritual insight stir to devotion and endeavor towards the highest life we can live. They show in every way and always the strong influence of Christian thought over her own mind and heart, and point always to that life which was revealed to the world in the coming of the Christ. She desired to live, and sought to have others live, the life of a devoted and loyal Christian.

How widely her influence as a teacher extended is seen in the fact that during a period of over thirty-five years she taught classes in Groton, Littleton, Townsend, Boston, Worcester, Dorchester, Norfolk, Va., Kalamazoo, Mich., and New London, N. H., and was Lady Principal in five important educational institutions. The remarkably symmetrical development of her mind and the variety of its powers is made evident by the statement that at different times during this period she taught the following branches of learning: Rhetoric, English Composition, Algebra, Physical Geography, Chemistry, Geology, Astronomy, Botany, Latin, German, Italian, English Literature, Drawing and Painting, Political Economy, Evidences of Christianity, Butler's Analogy, Paley's

Natural Theology, Mental and Moral Philosophy. It is surely no common experience to find such widely different branches of study successfully taught by the same teacher. And her ability to teach them was a far more significant fact thirty or forty years ago than it would be to-day.

She had also the eye of the artist and poet for everything beautiful. An artist herself, whether she painted in oil or water-color, upon silk or china, her work, especially in her favorite subjects, landscapes and flowers, was characterized by its delicacy of touch, its purity of color, and its careful finish.

But I have detained you by this tribute already too long; for, in planning this service, I was desirous that you should share with me the rich and rare privilege of having our dearly beloved friend speak to us out of her own writings,—a teacher's message. This will tell us far better of her life and character. This will show far better than I can describe them the nature and variety of her gifts. This will speak to us of her eager search for wisdom and her thirst for truth, the treasures of her mind, her devotion to her calling, the purity of her heart, the keenness of her spiritual vision, her sources of strength and power, her love for her Heavenly Father, the true nobility and beauty of her inspiring life. And if her message shall have that influence over you which it has already had over so many lives in the past,— Miss Dodge, if this commemoration ever comes to her knowledge, and he who reverently and gratefully pays this tribute to her greatness, will again before the face of God thank him for his bountiful gifts to this rare and beautiful soul among the children of men, and ascribe all praises to him forever.

SELECTIONS IN POETRY.

OH! I WOULD LIVE IN VISIONS!

Oh! I would live in visions! grant me visions
bright and fair,
Grant me to live in other worlds where I'd be free
from care.
I'd clothe in brilliant rainbow hues all the dull
scenes of life;
I'd dance with elves in fairy rings with pleasure
ever rife.

If happiness can ne'er be found, oh! why refuse
to dream,
And picture many happy scenes while sailing down
life's stream.
And if the dream be all a dream, why, let me dream
again;
I'd rather dream of being blest, than be alive to
pain.

Oh! I would live in visions high! visions of perfect bliss,
And I would find in spirit land the boon denied
in this.
I'd talk with beings fair and bright on ev'ry hill
and dale;
I'd listen to the murmuring tones of many a
wondrous tale.

I'd see a fairy in a flower, a naiad in the stream;
I'd hear the zephyr's whispered tale, 't would not
  be all a dream.
I'd hear the words the thunder speaks, and what
  the whirlwind tells;
I'd list the music of the spheres like chime of
  ev'ning bells.

Then let me live in visions! live in visions bright
  and fair!
Let me but soar above the earth and dwell in
  realms of air;
Let me forget all care awhile and e'en in dreams
  be blest.
Since we who travel life's rough way in visions
  can find rest. 1845-50.

ALL THINGS SPEAK TO ME.

I LOVE the fresh and balmy air
  That breathes o'er hill and lea.
That fans my brow and waves my hair;
  It speaks to me.

I love the clear and joyous light,
  That streams o'er earth and sea.
That decks the sky in beauty bright;
  It speaks to me.

I love the clouds in mountains piled.
  Or floating light and free,
And when they frown in tempests wild;
  They speak to me.

I love the forest's solemn tone.
  Its wild, demoniac glee,
Its laugh of joy, or sorrow's moan;
  It speaks to me.

I love the wild bird's mellow songs,
    That burst from shrub and tree.
While echo every note prolongs;
    It speaks to me.

I love the cup of dewy flower.
    I seem its smile to see.
And all its transitory hour;
    It speaks to me.

I love to gaze in silence deep
    On helpless infancy,
And while the angels vigil keep.
    It speaks to me.

I love the stars, the sea, the land:
    Tho' full of mystery,
Their voice I seem to understand —
    All speak to me.
                                1848.

ALL THINGS SMILE.

When fills the heart with joy and hope.
    And peace expands the brow,
When love the nature hath sublimed,
    And lofty thoughts endow,

All nature sends a kind response
    From every form she owns,
Reflects our smiles with loving face.
    Returns our joyous tones.

Skies, earth and sea, with smiling eye,
    Look down into the soul,
While draughts of gladness we may quaff,
    More sweet than nectared bowl.

The birds laugh forth their song of glee;
  The flocks and herds accord:
Each human face smiles happily,
  And work with joy is stored.

Then, radiant Peace, illume my soul,
  And Hope and Joy and Love,
'Till all my thoughts are beautiful
  With brightness from above.   1848–49.

NATURE.

A SPIRIT breathes from off this scene
  Of quiet, calm repose,
And floats in mist of silvery sheen
  Which round its drapery throws.

A voice comes from the woodland wild,
  A voice of meaning deep;
It calls above the earth-born child,
  It bids fierce passion sleep.

Oh, let me soar in thought away,
  Obey th' inviting voice,
And burst the bonds of cum'brous clay,
  With Nature's soul rejoice.

My soul would float in sunbeams bright
  Upon the wavy air,
Drink rapture from th' enchanting sight,
  Of angels pure and fair.

I see them now, I feel their power,
  My spirit leaves her clay;
Celestial radiance gilds the hour,
  I soar with them away.   1845–47.

THE IDEAL IN NATURE.

What is the earth? A dull, cold, lifeless thing:
The cloudy sky hangs o'er its leaden wing;
The ocean tosses with a sullen roar
Its angry waves upon a rocky shore.

The forests frown, and toss their threat'ning arms.
The bogs and ditches lie devoid of charms,
The hills their jagged, unformed fronts obtrude.
The plains stretch out a weary longitude.

Lo! this is all the man of sense beholds;
Nature to him no charm or grace unfolds;
But to the man of soul nought is all real,
All nature's forms are robed in bright ideal.

Earth's features rude, gleam with the light of life.
And trees and flowers with springs of joy are rife:
The birds and insects sing a song of glee,
And beasts and creeping things hold jubilee.

The radiant sky reflects the smile of God;
His voice, the ocean's roar and thunder loud:
The tall trees giants seem, by him endowed,
The trembling pilgrim safely to o'er shroud.

1847-48.

SMILES OF EDEN.

The preacher at church, in the sermon to-day,
Said, Eden from earth had long since passed away;
Said, Paradise fled at the first man's foul sin,
And sorrow and death had since then entered in.

The preacher was right in his words of to-day,
For Paradise long has from earth passed away,
But ling'ring it casts its sweet smiles all around,
On hillside, on glen, and on mountain they're found.

They gleam from the sky in the evening's bright
    hue,
When scarlet and gold softly blend with the blue;
When peep out the stars like the eye of a bride,
And th' moon leads her train in her matronly pride.

They shine on the brow of the innocent child
When joyful in sports his loud laugh rings out wild;
The angels oft speak to his unspotted heart,
Where malice and envy not yet find a part.

They're felt in the union of true loving souls,
And brighten, like sunlight, life's threatening
    shoals;
They glow in the glance of the child's trusting love
He caught from the host of pure spirits above.

And smiles from bright Eden are seen when the sire
Is kneeling at morn with devotion's pure fire,
And prays the blest Spirit on loved ones to rest,
And fill the desires of each suppliant breast.

Yes, traces of Eden are seen all around;
They gleam from the sky and are strewn on the
    ground;
They dwell in the heart and they rest on the brow;
Oh! Eden's fair flowers are blossoming now!

                                   1845-47.

WRITTEN ON A SPRING-LIKE DAY IN MID WINTER.

OH! the bright buds of Hope that are swelling
   From the depths of the dreamy mist,
And the sweet springs of joy that are welling
   From the earth that the sun has kissed.

For the Queen of the Spring is a-smiling,
   Through the chill of the winter's snows,
And our hearts with a promise beguiling,
   While a glimpse of her face she shows.

For she whispers of soft April showers,
   Of the flowers of May and June,
Of the fragrant and green summer bowers,
   With the birds and breezes in tune.

And her smile is the storm king subduing,
   And his voice to a love note tamed;
Oh! prolonged be the hours of their wooing,
   And her power be long maintained!

For with rapture our bosoms are beating,
   As the spring looks forth from the sky,
Though we know that the glance must be fleeting,
   Till the winter's long reign goes by.

                          JAN. 8, 1855.

SONG OF THE INDIAN SUMMER SPIRITS.

DREAMILY, blissfully, floating along,
Pillowed on zephyrs and lulled by their song,
Coming from homes in the isles of the blest,
Breathing o'er mortals the perfume of rest.

Down through the mists of the soft wavy air,
Sunshine of Eden, we smile on your care,
Telling of realms where all sorrow shall cease,
Lulling all spirits from turmoil to peace.

Coming to earth ere the death of the year,
Like a bright vision the dying to cheer,
Promising spring when the winter is gone,
Showing a glimpse of the hastening dawn.

Dreamily, blissfully, float we away,
Wooed by your longings we gladly would stay;
Tarried we only that visions of rest
Cheer your sad hearts from the isles of the blest.

Nov. 7, 1857.

THE LOVER'S JUBILATE.

O BEAUTIFUL, beautiful world!
    Sunbeams are flashing,
    Waters are dashing,
    Birds sweet are singing,
    Heaven's arch is ringing
With the beauty and music of earth.

O beautiful, beautiful life!
    Joys are upspringing,
    Hopes bright are singing,
    Faith's wings are soaring,
    Love is adoring;
Oh, the bliss and the rapture of life!

June 21, 1857.

THE ORGAN.

Now the temple's walls are raised,
   Now the shelt'ring roof is done,
Points the spire to God the praised,
   Open doors invite to come.

Human hearts with love are swelling
   To the God of earth and heaven;
Human tongues are eager telling
   Of the blessings he has given.

But not only creatures living
   To his praise their tribute bring;
Senseless matter, too, is giving
   Honor to the heavenly King.

For the organ's tones are pealing,
   And we breathe its breath of praise;
Through the aisles and arches stealing,
   Stones and wood an anthem raise.

Soft, anon, the strain is telling
   All the sinner's grief and woe;
All the deep emotion welling
   When the contrite boweth low.

All the struggling, all the anguish,
   All the gloomy doubts and fears,
When the fainting soul doth languish,
   And no voice of comfort hears.

Sweetly now melodious numbers
   Come like sunshine through the shower,
Like new life from death's dark slumbers,
   Like bright Hope in Sorrow's hour.

Peace and Love are softly wreathing
  Sweetest strains of deep delight,
And we hush our very breathing,
  Awed before the organ's might.

Now more rapturous tones are pealing
  All harmonious on the ear,
Joys of Paradise revealing,
  No discordant grief or fear.

Ceased the strain, yet, soaring, sinking,
  Hovers yet in fancy round;
Wondrous is the organ, linking
  Deepest thought with solemn sound!

AUGUST, 1855.

RECANTATION.

AGAIN I seize the lyre,
  Too long its strings are mute;
Now move with minstrel's fire,
  My eager heart, my lute:

Of "visions high" speak, speak again,
  That in my soul have dwelt:
"High purpose" sound in bolder strain
  That this weak heart hath felt.

Repeat the thoughts that scald my brain,
  That drink my spirit's life;
Vibrate to wretchedness and pain,
  To life's fierce toil and strife.

Inspire with purpose dutiful,
  And yearnings for the good,
With meltings at the beautiful
  In river, sky, and wood.

Be silent when the spirit land
    Its wonders shows to me:
Be silent while th' angelic band
    Reveal Heaven's harmony.

Let, O my lyre, this aching heart
    Vent its wild throbs on thee;
When tears from my pressed eyelids start
    Oh, come to comfort me.

And when I rise to smile on Fate,
    And the good angels reign,
When Love on smiling Peace doth wait,
    Oh, then send forth thy strain.

1848.

TO A STAR.

UNMEASURED the path to that dim distant star,
How faint is its light that beams cold from afar;
Tho' long is the way that mild star beam has
    trod,
It has spoken to me of the power of God.

It shines in my heart and enkindles a flame
That lightens life's trackless and uncertain main;
It tells me that He who has guided this beam
Will direct all my way howe'er dark it may seem.

Oh, then I'll cast doubting and sorrow away,
I'll think when 't is night of the soon coming day;
I'll trust in the God who is mighty to save
From the trials of earth and the power of the
    grave.

1845-48.

THOUGHTS AT EVENTIDE.

I am alone — no sound of human voice,
Or gentle footstep, falls upon my ear
To tell me aught else lives, and nature's calm
Hath entered my lone heart. The mellow light
Hath spread its splendor where so oft the storm
Or whirlwind reigned; the misty evening air
Waves gently now with balmy fragrance in
Its light embrace, and I am all alone.
Yet not alone can the free spirit be
At such an hour. Methinks I see the dear,
Sweet countenance of friends, those whom my
    heart
Holds dear, now look on me with shadowy yet
Familiar eyes; the gaze of soul into
Its kindred soul, without a veil between.

I'm not alone — for pillowed on the air,
Or sporting free in joyous harmony,
Are myriads of spirits all around,
Who beckon me from sordid earthliness.
I'm not alone! another Spirit's here!
The Comforter, the Holy Influence
That leads me to adore and humbly bow.
My spirit melts; the sun among the stars
Eclipses all, — God, God alone is here,
And friends and spirits all are lost in him.

1845-48.

FROM MY HEART — A MOOD.

How longs my lonely soul for sympathy!
Oh, for a friend of mine in whose kind ear
I might pour out the secrets of my heart!

My feelings leap and long for utterance,
There is no kindred soul to whom I may
Unfold the longings of my saddened heart.
Sometimes I do forget, and speak myself,
But no one lists to me — they say I dream
When telling them of my realities.
No one I meet who understands. Perhaps
The fault is mine, for I do fear mankind,
And I have almost learned to wear the mask
Which the unthinking world do ever wear.
Sometimes I think that I am not myself,
And listen to the old philosophers
Who taught that such a fancy might be true.
But still I feel that I am all alone;
No heart with mine in blessèd sympathy
Doth beat. Some think me wise, and many more
Brand fool, or one they ne'er can comprehend:
When I am sad, some loss of paltry gold
Is guessed to be the cause, and when I smile
It is because some fool has smiled on me.
But these things are — and true philosophy
Doth sternly bid me take the ills of life.
"The ills of life" have never reached me yet:
But mine are sorrows of the inmost soul
For which the wordlings ne'er have found a name.
Sometimes Ambition rules with iron rod,
And bids me stand upon the heights of fame.
I long for fame, for love, and for applause;
Receiving none, I mourn in secret place.
I care not for the praise of stolid fools,
Or undeserved applause from any lip:
But I'd deserve the love of great and good,
And strive to merit what may be withheld.
Ambition gives but to destroy bright hopes
Till, wearied with her wiles, her subjects seek
For some lone wilderness where human foot

Hath ne'er disturbed the fresh, unfingered moss.
To live and die unknown. But oh, I wish
To wear the favored scholar's well-earned wreath:
To search the hidden lore of ages through,
And claiming Virtue, Wisdom, as my friend,
My guide, live known to Fame, or hidden in
My lone retreat,— my soul will ask no more.

MAY, 1843.

THE RIDE.

GIVE me my fleet and comely steed,
  My jetty steed for me;
With flowing mane o'er curvèd neck,
  And nostril spreading free.

I list to his impatient hoof,
  He calls me with his neigh:
He longs, as I, to slip the noose,
  And bound in glee away.

He curbs his spirit while I mount,
  Then chafes and spurns the rein,
And, sportive, threats to throw me hence,
  And laughs to find it vain.

Now let us bound, my steed, away
  From homes of care-worn men;
We'll seek free spirits like our own
  O'er hills or shaded glen.

Oh, give me, then, my sable steed,
  That dear loved steed for me,
With flowing mane and curvèd neck,
  And nostril spreading free.

1848.

WHAT IS MAN?

A LONELY pilgrim on a desert drear,
Wearied and sad, oppressed with nameless fear.
Hung'ring and thirsty, no oasis near;
    Such, such is man!

A trembling slave in iron fetters bound,
Whom tyrant masters trample to the ground.
Helpless to heed bright Freedom's joyful sound:
    Such, such is man!

A toil-worn laborer 'neath a crushing load,
Climbing at noon a steep and rocky road,
Where ne'er the streams of joy or hope have
    flowed;
    Such, such is man!

A soldier, constant 'mid the battle's roar,
Who long has fought, nor e'er the victory bore,
Who dares not hope the strife will e'er be o'er;
    Such, such is man!

A prophet who can read his hast'ning doom,
Who sees before him but the yawning tomb,
And scarcely there the bones of friends make
    room;
    Such, such is man!

Heaven's heir is man, the loving God, when known,
Will bear his load, adopt him as his own,
Clothe him in kingly robes, place on his throne;
    Even such is man!

                          1852.

THE PAUPER'S FUNERAL.

Now the last rites are said,
To his cold, narrow bed
　　Bear him away.
Fierce blows the wintry blast,
Snow wreaths around are cast.
　　But speed your way.

Oft in his life unblest,
Longed he for place of rest,
　　Bear ye him on.
No friend will bid you stay,
Bear the poor man away
　　Ere set of sun.

Hope once his heart beguiled,
And love upon him smiled,
　　Life's scenes were bright.
Hope turned her face away,
Love lived but one short day,
　　And then was night!

From heart to heart he turned,
For each his spirit yearned,
　　But all were dumb.
Then lone, deserted, drear,
Waited some word of cheer
　　Till death should come.

But, earth's best glories shorn,
Then heavenly joys were born,
　　Stars gemmed his night.
To-day for him no stars;
Heaven's golden gate unbars
　　And floods their light.

　　　　　　　JUNE 20, 1857.

MORNING HYMN.

To thee, our Father, would we bring
    Our first glad song of praise;
Thou hast the gloomy night dispelled
    And sent the morning rays.

With morn's glad light come cheering hopes,
    And swell the exulting soul;
We bless thy kind, indulgent hand,
    Dispenser of the whole.

Our skies no clouds or darkness show,
    But rainbow hues instead;
Fresh flowers with fragrant beauty strew
    The path wherein we tread.

And when our sun has run his course,
    And shut the gates of day,
May those of heavenly homes invite
    Our wearied spirit's stay.

                          TOWNSEND, 1852.

EVENING HYMN.

THUS far upon Life's winding way
Have clouds and sunshine marked the day.—
Forward, the path seems rough and steep,
And older pilgrims mourn and weep.

They tell of dangers they've passed by,
And warn us of destruction nigh:
The thorn and noxious herb they show,
The lofty crags and pitfalls low.

Kind Father, take us by the hand,
And lead us through this frowning land;
Let us not lone in darkness roam,
While seeking for our heavenly home.

From Pleasure's flowers turn us aside,
From riches, honor, fame, and pride:
May " Wisdom's way " our souls allure,
And grant us wealth which shall endure.

And when grim Death our frame awaits,
May angels open th' pearly gates;
May our blest spirits enter in
Where dwells no sorrow, death, nor sin.

TOWNSEND, 1852.

SONG. (INSCRIBED TO J. T.)

How pure and delightful the pleasure
  These happy young faces to see!
How better than gold or rich treasure
  The echo of glad tones of glee!

There's naught upon earth that can move us
  Like childhood's approaches to bliss;
The angels in bright groups above us
  See nothing more lovely than this.

How blest are the hearts that remember
  To whom much is given must give,
And they who with open hands render
  To God again gifts they receive.

May blessings of Heaven attend him,
  His heart, and his home, and his gold,
Who blesseth the children, whose angels
  Do always the Father behold.

1863.

THE HOURS, PAST, PRESENT, AND FUTURE.

Tableau and Recitation at Codman Hill, July 10, 1863.

(Suggested by a Picture in the Providence Athenæum.)

PRESENT. All of joy I bring with me,
    Only in my smile ye live;
In my hand all blessings see,
    From my stores all good receive.

FUTURE. Joyous hopes with me reside,
    All the light of coming years;
Ne'er with me doth grief abide,
    Ne'er with me are sighs and tears.

PAST. In my treasury, garnering all,
    Hold I all that life has given;
Ne'er from me in vain ye call
    Scenes of bliss and hours of heaven.

FUTURE. All the Past is drear and dead,
Present joys are quickly fled;
Still the Future beckons one,
"Live ye in to-morrow's sun."

PRESENT. Clouds may veil the morrow's sun,
Hopelessly the Past is done;
Only ye the Now possess,
Only I may really bless.

PAST. Grief and pain the Present bears,
Frowns the Future often wears;
Gather from my stores with skill,
Leave all sorrow, if ye will.

PRESENT.	All the treasures of past ages,
	Borne along with mighty power.
	All the Future bright presages
	Join to crown the Present hour.
PAST.	By the Past the Present standeth,
	By the Past the Future gleams;
	Ne'er the Past its force disbandeth,
	Ne'er are quenched its setting beams.
FUTURE	Past and Present from me drawing,
	Gather life from age to age;
	All Eternity's enjoying
	Seek ye in my opening page.
ALL.	Ne'er can meet we sisters three,
	Daughters of Eternity;
	Ne'er can view a sister's face,
	Pausing in our endless race.
	We each other's voices hear
	Calling from afar and near;
	Ne'er on common ground we stand,
	Yet are clasping hand in hand.
	Time shall end, earth cease to be,
	Yet shall live we sisters three.

SONG FOR REUNION OF THE NORTH SCHOOL, LITTLETON, MASS.

TUNE.—"Auld Lang Syne."

SHOULD North School comrades be forgot,
And days when we were young?
Should North School mem'ries fade away?
And ne'er be told or sung?

CHORUS. — For old North School, my friends,
    For old North School;
    We'll take each other by the hand,
    For old North School.

We long have roamed about the world,
    And ta'en our share of toil;
We've wandered many a weary mile
    Since on our native soil.
CHORUS. — For old North School, etc.

We will not pledge in brimming cup
    Of treacherous, maddening wine,
But here's a hand, my trusty friend,
    Gi'e us a hand of thine.
CHORUS. — For old North School, etc.

                1885.

THE ERL KING.

(From the German.)

The Erl King is a mischievous and malignant being in the mythology of the ancient Germans. This piece is the opening of one of Goethe's operas.

WHO rides so late in this tempest so wild?
'T is the bold father braves the dark night with his
    child.
His fond arm is strong, and no fear dims his eye,
Safe holds he the boy as homeward they fly.

"My son, what fear'st thou, why hid'st thou thy
    sight?"
"O father! look forth in the deep of the night;
The Erl King! the Erl King! with train and with
    crown!"
"The evening mist's gloom in the distance, my
    son."

"Thou dear child, thou fair child, oh, come, go
 with me;
Many beautiful games will I play there with thee;
For thee my bright flowers their hues will unfold,
And my mother will deck thee in garments of
 gold."

"My father! my father! O listen! O hear!
What the Erl King promises low in my ear!"
" Be quiet, be quiet, my dear little child,
In the old oaks but rustles the winter wind wild!"

"Come! wilt thou, my dear boy, now go to my
 home?
My daughter will watch thee, and with thee will
 roam;
For thee fairy revels she nightly will keep,
She shall rock thee, and sing thee, and dance thee
 to sleep."

"My father! my father! and see'st thou not there
His daughter's dark form in the thick gloomy
 air?"
" My son, yes, my son, I see it now clear;
'T is the old willows gray in the darkness appear."

"I love thee, must have thee, as have thee I may;
I'll snatch thee, I'll bear thee with me far away."
" My father! my father! he's doing me harm!
The Erl King will tear me away from thy arm."

The bold father shudders, he spurs on his steed,
While trembles the child in his arms like a reed;
He reaches his cottage, with terror and dread,
And the beautiful boy in his arms is dead.

June, 1850.

MY GOLD AND MY JEWELS.

(*From the German.*)

In plenty I have gold,— 'tis the glorious dear
    sunshine,
As it glimmers through my window,— it is mine,
    wholly mine.

How wonderful and how noble is this my solar
    gold!
It brings to me no trouble and no fear of robber
    bold.

It doth warm me, it doth light me in my heart's
    deepest vein,
And when it shimmers friendly it comforts every
    pain.

In my dark and gloomy soul it brings the radiant
    day,
From the weeping morning flowers it doth kiss
    the tears away.

These flowers spring up for me in their gorgeous
    colors bright,
Their pure and fragrant beauty is the joyous
    Spring's delight.

From the sungold and the pearls in the still and
    solemn night —
We say it is the dew — are the lovely flowers
    bedight;

And their jewels of fine pearls and of fragrant
    gold are wrought,
Which, in dreamy slumber deep, to the flower
    world are brought.

With such jewels I ofttimes do my humble head
    adorn,
And in them I am richer than a prince to splendor
    born.

Then my wealth is always fruitful, it never fails
    in store,
For the flower jewels splendid each spring brings
    to my door.

THE IDEAL.
(From Schiller.)

So, faithless, wilt thou hence depart,
  With all thy friendly visions bright,
With all thy sorrows, all thy joys,
  And ne'er retrace thy distant flight?
Can naught restrain thy wingèd car
  O golden hours of youth's gay dream?
In vain I call — thy waters clear
  Haste to Eternity's dark stream.

Extinguished are the stars of hope,
  Which sparkled o'er my youthful way,
The visions of ideal good
  That once could my weak heart betray;
Departed is the sweet, fond trust
  My youthful dream in Being gave,—
Life's beauty and divinity
  In the rough Actual find their grave.

As once with fervent, longing prayer,
  Pygmalion to the statue knelt,
Until the glow of life and love
  On the cold cheek of marble dwelt;
So with an eager, youthful love,
  Enshrined I Nature in my breast,
Until she breathed, she warmed with life,
  At the bold poet's high behest.

Rewarding then my ardent zeal,
   E'en Silence found herself a tongue,
Gave back to me my kiss of love,
   Responded as my pulses rung.
Then glowed with life the tree, the flower,
   Then sang to me the bright cascade;
All senseless things had found a soul
   Which echoed all my fancy made.

So from one struggling, conquering breast
   The single soul to all went forth.
With faith in all that life portrayed
   Of purpose high and deeds of worth.
A spacious world in his high dreams,
   As shrouded in the embryo rolled;
Alas! how slow to his bright hopes
   Did all its hidden powers unfold.

No sad reverse as yet had curbed
   The youth upon his path of life;
Blessed was he still in blissful dreams,
   Winged with bold zeal he sought the strife.
E'en to the stars in ether pure
   The swarms of his designs uprose,
And naught so high and naught so far
   Which could his restless flight oppose.

How lightly was he borne along;
   What shadow glooms on Fortune's child!
How danced before his triumph car
   The airy train with pleasure wild!
Love, smiling to his longing gaze,
   Fortune, with wreath of golden light,
Fame, with her crown of fadeless stars,
   And Truth, with robes of sunshine bright.

But lo! the goal not half attained,
  Dispersed were his companions gay;
Too soon they turned their faithless steps,
  And one by one they fled away.
Fortune departed, light of foot,
  And, as his thirst of knowledge grew,
Thick clouds of gloomy doubt concealed
  The sunny form of Truth from view.

I saw the sacred crown of Fame
  Upon the vulgar brow, profaned,
And all too quick the springtime gone,
  When Love with witching smiles remained.
More still, more lone, the scene became,
  And steeper grew the rough ascent,
While scarce one glimmering ray of hope
  My path its friendly radiance lent.

Of all the bustling retinue
  Which by me stood the journey through?
Which travelled, trusting, by my side,
  E'en with the gates of death in view?
Friendship, with thy soft, gentle hand,
  'T was thou who healedst every wound,
Who, loving, half life's burden bore,
  Thou, whom I early sought and found!

And thou, who joined with Friendship's balm,
  As it my spirit's storm had calmed,
Blest Labor, with thy slow rewards,
  Hast all my weary moments charmed;
Thou, from eternity's vast store,
  Dost grant us only grain by grain,
Yet from the mighty debt of time,
  Minutes, and days, and years dost drain.

APRIL 11, 1855.

SELECTIONS IN PROSE.

TALKS TO HER PUPILS.

I. — SELF-GOVERNMENT.

"ORDER is Heaven's first law." We see this great principle prevailing everywhere throughout the works of the Great Architect. Everything has its due dependence on some other part of creation. We see system within system, and sequence linked with sequence, and all moving on in the most perfect harmony. There is no confusion among the heavenly bodies by planets or suns wandering from their courses. The idea that all the systems of worlds move harmoniously around some common centre is entirely analogous to what we see in other departments of creation. Even in "the little part we dimly scan" we see in the various classes of created objects a tendency to supremacy in some one. We speak of the lordly oak of the forest; of the queenly rose of our gardens; of the eagle as the king of birds; of the lion as the undisputed monarch among beasts. It would indeed be singular if the analogy failed when applied to men. And it does not, for the necessity of subordination is felt from the very first stages of society. But we need not look to classes of men, to nations, to communities, or even to families and schools, but may find within our own breasts illustrations of this principle.

Our own passions, emotions, and faculties of mind may be compared to a nation of separate individuals, which, without some head, some controlling principle, will rush madly on to their own destruction, leading misery and anarchy in their train. It is of self-government that I desire to speak. And what among our faculties or impulses must we regard as worthy of supreme authority, with which we may invest royal power? Among the powers of the mind the will is the director. We may express the right condition of this in a few words; it should be identified with the will of God. The other faculties may bring to it the knowledge of his will, as the subjects of a despot may report to him tidings to regulate his acts, but human will itself should be but an echo of that of the Sovereign of the universe. And how may his will be known? He has given us reason and conscience to learn his designs, and to direct our actions. Human will alone, though it must prompt every act, is but a fickle and arbitrary despot, unfit to rule without being itself ruled by an enlightened conscience and rightly directed reason. God, in giving us a will of our own, has placed in our hands the power of rightly training our various faculties, of using them in a way to promote the greatest amount of happiness to ourselves, and performing the greatest amount of good to others. Or we may, by wilful ignorance, or a careless perversion of these faculties, bring misery to ourselves and injury to others.

We are responsible, as far as our means of information have extended, for the proper development of our physical nature. This part of our being is under the control of physical laws which it is the duty of every reasonable being to obey. There is a singular state of feeling on the subject of obedience to this class of the laws of our nature which has led to much suffering and sin. Many individuals who would not knowingly violate the least point of moral law recklessly tread upon the plainest requirements of their physical nature. As if a law of God might be disregarded innocently, whether to be learned from the pages of inspiration or from the observation of causes and effects in the natural world. As though the partaking of articles of food known to be injurious, or tempting others with the same, were innocent, while suicide and murder are crimes of blackest dye. Govern yourselves, rise above your impulses, and pursue the course marked out by the higher faculties.

Our intellectual nature is a subject of discipline and control. The human mind is as a vast field, where weeds and brambles will grow in luxuriance unless the hand of cultivation interpose and convert the whole into a blooming garden. It is like the unbroken colt, useless until brought into subjection. The power of disciplining the faculties is within ourselves. We may place ourselves in favorable circumstances for this training, but the contest is within. Our faculties, to be of the greatest use, should be manageable. When we wish the mind to act, if properly trained, it will obey us, and we can go calmly about the appointed task, sure that the desired results will be accomplished. "The perfection of a disciplined mind is, not to be able on some great contingency to rouse up its faculties and draw out a giant strength, but to have it always ready to produce a given, adequate quantity of results in a given and equal time." You can, by comparing yourself now with what you were months or years ago (those of you who are really students), probably perceive that you have much more power over yourself than at that time: you can more easily confine your attention to a given point and "think it out." You do not find so much difficulty in following a discussion or planning a piece of written composition. Let this encourage you to proceed in the work of mental discipline. New victories will daily be gained by the resolute will. The conquest itself is full of delight to the determined soul, and the result of the victory an advantage never to be lost. The more active and vigorous your powers, the more the need of self-government, as the more powerful the subjects of a king, the more energetic should be his reign, to prevent violent and tumultuous outbreaks. Let, then, your first object be to make your mind obey you, to make your powers submit to reason.

Man, as a moral being, needs self-control. Many are the temptations to sin, in thought as well as in word and act. He needs a principle within which shall command and be obeyed. Those lawless rovings of the imagination which lead to sin must be checked. Sin tempts in a thousand forms. The allurements it holds out are fitted to entice those of every age and condition. The student, though secluded from the attractions of the busy world, yet finds constant need of moral courage and stern self-control to keep from even outward sin. And the temptations to sin, which can be known only to the all-seeing eye, how numerous! I have named the power of resistance, self-control. Yet who that has tried the experiment but has found himself unequal to the test, but has felt the need of something without on which to depend? Who has not felt the need of a power superior to his own will, with its directors to control the whole? The perfection of self-government is an entire reliance on the government of God, the all-wise controller of the universe, and a bringing of all our powers into accordance with his requirements.

This discipline of the mind and heart is one great end of education. Scholars, even those who have made some little progress in their education, are apt to forget this, and ask the benefit of a course of disciplinary study. They say they will have no use in after life for this particular branch, and will perhaps forget the whole. Be it so. They cannot help being profited if they have diligently and laboriously studied. The power which has been gained over the attention, the exertion of the powers to grasp the difficult subject, are sufficient reward for its pursuit. Of what use are the particular exercises of the gymnasium, if not to develop and strengthen the muscular powers of the body? A writer who made the education of youth his business and study once said: "If your teachers should put you to studying magic, take hold and study it without quarrelling with it. There may be no practical use in it, but the discipline of mind required by wading through an intricate subject is of immense value."

Remember, then, that no effort of the mind is ever lost; though it may not be rewarded in just the way you expected, it will certainly prepare you to make another effort more powerful and better directed. Fear not to bring your mind to grapple with great and intricate subjects. In no other way can it be prepared for great achievements. In no other way can it take its stand among other educated minds with any show of equality.

A subjugation of all our powers to the dominion of reason and conscience is the best means of promoting our own happiness and that of others. It cannot have escaped the observation of anyone that those who allow themselves to be governed by their impulses, who act as present inclination prompts, are continually bringing upon themselves troubles which the more calm and philosophical entirely escape. There is, in ill-regulated minds, ever a restlessness, an uneasiness, craving some stimulus, and incapable of acting resolutely upon anything. The natural state of the faculties is activity. Happiness is found in the exercise of our powers. If these powers be not directed to appropriate objects, they turn upon themselves, and, like the miserable wretches in Dante's vision, lacerate and worry each other. A well-regulated mind never waits for employment. Subjects of interest for investigation are constantly before it. It seeks for knowledge as its appropriate food, and demands also daily fresh supplies. The possessor of such a mind would as soon think of fasting a day or a week as of neglecting to add some new idea to his mental storehouse for the same length of time. The anecdote of the philosopher who rose, after having retired at night, on being able to recollect no knowledge gained during the day, illustrates the assertion.

It is, perhaps, unnecessary to attempt to prove that the person of self-control is more capable of promoting the happiness of others than the opposite character. Who can enjoy the society of one to-day in raptures, to-morrow in tears, one day a friend, the next a foe, and ready at all times to give way to the most extravagant whims; the mood never at any time to be calculated upon. What parent can take delight in a daughter who will needlessly bring disease upon herself in the indulgence of a vitiated appetite or careless exposure to changes of temperature. What hours of anxiety does such a daughter cause many a fond mother, which a few moments reflection on her own part might prevent. How much more satisfaction can a teacher take in that pupil always to be depended on, than in one who is well prepared "only when she feels like it." And how much more happiness can all the friends of a young lady feel in contemplating her as one who can govern her desires, who can resist temptations to evil, whose whole character is based on principles of moral rectitude, than in one for whom they must always fear, and concerning whom they can never feel at ease when "out of their sight."

A sufficient motive for the exercise of self-government will be found in the consideration of its being a duty. We may see the will of the Creator in this by tracing the results of our actions. We may find, too, precepts concerning it in Holy Writ. Paul spoke of the necessity of keeping his body in subjection, and his thoughts under government. There is every motive to urge to this self-subjugation. There is a false pride which sometimes rebels against obeying the commands of another, but cannot against obeying one's self. There is a feeling of satisfaction in every victory over one's evil propensities. There is a feeling of happiness in becoming each day more as we should be, and reflecting that we ourselves are the doers of the work. The truly noble mind will thankfully receive every aid possible to be afforded in so important a work; but still it must mainly be performed by each for himself. The greatest victories are those one gains over himself. How many who have conquered empires have never gained such a victory. Yet it may be won by the humblest and weakest who really makes the attempt.

II. — Industry.

The importance of active, industrious habits to man as promotive of health and cheerfulness is such that it may almost be doubted whether the curse pronounced on Adam has not been converted into a blessing. Where shall we look for the various forms of disease in their greatest number if not among the idle? Where shall we find the dull, sluggish eye, and hear of sadness and lowness of spirits, if not among those whose minds feed on vacuity and pine in their emptiness? A proper exercise both of mind and body is necessary to the full development of either, and in the due exercise of their several faculties may be found the highest degree of happiness. We cannot doubt the design of our Creator in this respect. We see that he connects happiness with industry, as well as makes it the means of man securing to himself the comforts and conveniences of life. Man was not created like the wild beast of the forest, with garments of hair or fur to protect him from the inclemency of the weather, or so formed as to endure the changes of temperature without a defence reared about him. But he has been placed amid circumstances calculated to develop his energies, to call forth constantly the powers of his mind, which, if not exercised in preparing to meet the exigencies of his situation, must be followed by the suffering and death of himself, and those depending on him. The mind, too, was not endowed with an intuitive perception of all which it desired to know, but was surrounded with objects to excite curiosity, one of its most active powers. The mind was formed for activity, for industry, without which it must be a blank, where sin will write in dark and effaceless characters.

Industrious habits are of peculiar importance to women. They are of importance to her first, because of the many duties devolving upon her. During her whole life, the virtuous woman may say "she has more than she knows how to do." As a daughter residing under the parental roof, she need never be idle. She may make her services valuable to her mother by assisting her in her domestic cares, and thus preparing herself for future life, while she may, if she possesses brothers and sisters, do much to render home attractive to them, as well as be actively engaged for their welfare and improvement. She will not think, because not summoned imperatively from her couch at an early hour, that she may indefinitely prolong the morning sleep; but the thought of unperformed duties will call her betimes to their performance. She will not lounge listlessly on the sofa, or saunter in an aimless walk, while her mother is weighed down with her oppressive labors. She will not spend hours in idleness, while her wardrobe is ready to cry out for shame of its neglected condition. She will not call a servant from a distant part of the house to do that for her which a slight exertion of her own would have easily accomplished. She will not show, in any instance, that she considers it honorable to have nothing to do, and will not dare boast of her inactive and useless life. If her circumstances are such that she is not compelled to labor for herself with her hands, she will still find enough to do in the cultivation of her mind, and in works of charity. As a scholar, industry is absolutely necessary to proficiency. There is no "royal road" to science. Whoever would become familiar with its truths must himself labor, and assiduously, too. The remark is perhaps a trite one that persevering application is more valuable to the student with ordinary powers than a lively and fertile genius without it. To you as students, then, I would speak. The rough and shapeless marble is before you; it depends upon you whether it ever take the form of a beautiful statue. With the most fixed determination, it is still but by stroke after stroke for day after day and month after month that aught can be accomplished. The hill of science is to be climbed, and it is only by rising early and sitting up late, tugging each moment at the toilsome ascent, hoping and trusting, though the advance be but step by step, that a high point will yet be reached. Think, as you commence the life of a student, that you have commenced a life of labor, one in which "avarice of time" must be felt or nothing can be done.

In order to accomplish the greatest amount as a scholar, the daily duties should be distinctly understood, and a plan formed to occupy the whole time. No delay should ever be made in deciding what to do next, but the finishing of one thing should immediately suggest the next. This plan should be strictly adhered to if possible. If broken in upon, contrive some way to make up the time lost. Do not lose the fragments of time, but let the improvement of these be a part of your plan. Decide what can best be done in them, and let them not be spent in idleness. Have at hand some needle-work of a character to demand little attention to attend to while conversing upon subjects and on occasions that do not demand the whole attention. Do not imagine, however, that your industry in intellectual pursuits is well repaid when you have succeeded in performing a great number of things. It is the depth to which you dig, rather than the surface you scratch over, which will prove the value of your labor. The purest gold is brought from the depth of the mine, the richest pearls are not thrown upon the shore for the careless wanderer to gather, but lie deep beneath old ocean's briny wave. Let your aim, then, be to search to the bottom of the subjects presented to you. It is a positive injury to attend to subjects without completely mastering them, though imagining that you are becoming proficients in them. Remember, to be a good scholar you must be an industrious one, and there is no calling which repays the laborer with a greater harvest of happiness. If the ascent be toilsome, flowers border the path. If the point in view be far above you, it is in a purer atmosphere and under fairer skies. If the road be steep, the helping hand of sages of old and of geniuses of the present is extended to help you, while voices of wisdom and inspiration are inviting you upward. Do not repine, then, at the difficulties in your path. They may each become a stimulus to goad you on.

The idea, though absurd, is not uncommon, that the training of the mental powers, which a young lady receives at school, is not of the least use to her as a wife. If her education has been worthy of the name, it has prepared her for her duties in that capacity. A well-balanced mind, with a sound judgment, adapts itself to the circumstances in which it is placed. So far from domestic duties being beneath the attention of a well-educated woman, she may find pleasure, and a call for no mean talent, in their performance. Some of our most gifted lady writers have busied themselves in them in the interim of literary labors, without fearing that the fumes of the kitchen would taint their admired productions. We find two opposite courses of conduct pursued by young ladies in regard to matrimony and its duties. One class make it the principal subject of thought and topic of conversation, showing, by actions at least, that they consider that the chief end of their existence is to be married; while another, properly disgusted with such conduct, and lamenting the ridicule to which their whole sex are exposed by it, fall into the opposite extreme, and think nothing of preparing themselves for the discharge of the duties of a state to which all may look forward as one proper for woman. This may seem foreign to my subject, but I wish to impress on your minds that the whole course of your future life will imperatively call for industrious habits, and from the multiplicity and importance of the cares of married life, they should not be assumed lightly, or without a preparation in the school of industry. I wish you to remember that the habits I urge upon you to acquire now are important to you as a preparation for the all-important future.

III. — Wisdom.

To proceed in the pursuit of knowledge and mental discipline is the true interest of every one. Nothing else will enable one to compete in the transaction of business with the foresighted and designing of the world. Nothing will command more respect from our fellow men. The gaudy trappings of wealth may command the homage of the interested and the ignorant, but this will draw the esteem of the wise and good. Knowledge is power. Nothing will give more influence, not only over vulgar and ignorant minds, but over equals and superiors. A powerful intellect may mould the multitude at its will, and stem the current of wrath and violence at its bidding.

Our talents are bestowed upon us for use. An account of them will be required of us, and it behooves us to see to it that we do not waste our Lord's money, but so manage it that it may be returned to him with usury. I do not hesitate to say that it is the duty of each one of you to strive to obtain the very best education the best institutions of our land will aid you in gaining, and to go forward in its pursuit when removed from the stimulus of instructors and classmates. You ought to let their motive influence you when toiling up the steep and rugged hill of science. Remember that you are in the path of duty, that you have the right on your side. Pecuniary difficulties, often so formidable to the best students, have as often been found by them not to be insuperable, but even the means of rousing the mind to greater exertions, and calling out otherwise hidden powers. To a mind roused to a sense of the importance of knowledge, and with a love of it, the mountains of the slothful and indifferent become mole-hills, and the lions in the way of the timid and fearful recede as the hare before the hounds of the hunter. Such a one may truly say that to him nothing "under the whole heaven has been found difficult," for his mind has been determined.

It is a real blessing to have intelligent correspondents. Next to that of social intercourse in the pleasure it confers, it is superior to it in many respects as a means of improvement. "Thought written is the more possessed." But letter writing alone might generate a too loose and illogical style and habit of thinking. Essays, discussions, dissertations, reviews, etc., should be written. Perhaps they may never meet the eye or approbation of another, and it is not for this purpose you should write them. They will discipline your own mind, and some of them, perchance, as time may have matured your powers, may be found worthy the perusal of the still insatiate public. They will be to your own soul their "exceeding great reward." You can trace by them your progress from year to year. From the small beginnings you now make you may advance to a high place among the authors of our land, "for to write aptly is of practice." "To be accurate, write; to remember, write; to know thine own mind, write."

But it is not in human nature to continue a course so laborious without something to cheer and encourage. What, then, has the student? What have you to encourage you in your pursuit of wisdom that you shall ever obtain the prize, or gain enough to repay you for your toils? You may be encouraged by looking to what others have done, with no superiority of talent, and with, perhaps, inferior facilities for cultivating it. When we contemplate the attainments of a More, a Lady Jane Gray, a Sigourney, or Hannah Adams, we are perhaps apt to imagine them superior in natural talent to ourselves. This may be true, but how do we know but that we may equal or even excel them if the effort be made and continued? I do not believe in an exclusiveness of talent. I see not why there may not be now in existence thousands unknown to fame who are every whit as highly endowed by nature as those whom the silver trump has so long delighted in proclaiming. I would not by this place fame before you as a thing to be desired or sought for; but would lead you to trust your powers, and labor with them to acquire the means of making yourself happy and useful to those around you. Your sphere of influence may be large or it may be small, but so far as it extends let it be of weight. You may be encouraged by the increased capacity of happiness your intellectual growth gives you. It is true there is an increased capacity of suffering; but we may, if we will, choose the beautiful, the good, and the true for our companions in the path of learning, and reject the gloomy espionage of Despondency, with her frowning brow and evil and false alarms.

To do good should be our object of living. How to do it, then, is a matter of no small importance. How many acts of intended kindness have, for want of knowledge, sent an arrow to the heart they meant to soothe! If we intend them to do good to our fellow men we must study their natures, and the more powerful the mind which we bring into action in this work, the more perfectly will it be done. Our knowledge may help us to instruct the ignorant, may devise means to satisfy the bodily wants, and may direct us in applying heaven-born truth to erring and suffering humanity. All culture of the intellect should be subservient to that of the moral powers. It should be so conducted as to draw them out, and pursued from motives which are bounded not by earth. We should consider the education of our powers as a preparation for eternity. I doubt not that the progress made here in knowledge influences our happiness in the future world, and that no acquirement will be lost. Our greatness of intellect will increase our happiness or enhance our woe.

In my view of such motives and ends, I would say to you, — Press on in the work of improvement. Look further and still further into the mysteries of the universe, and prepare to gaze far away into the immeasured depths of Deity. Oh, it is unearthly happiness to unloose the thoughts, and even while in the fetters of the flesh, soar away into the spiritual world, feeling our spirits assimilating, mingling with the purer essences of heaven. We have none of us more than walked along the coast of the vast sea of knowledge; perchance we have gathered a few pebbles from its shore, while far beyond in its unexplored depths lie pearls more rich than the Indian diver has ever dreamed of. Let us launch boldly upon its yet unmeasured extent: let us prepare for a long voyage upon its ever brightening waves, and fear not to dive deep that we may bring up its richest treasures.

"Oh press on!
For it shall make you mighty among men,
And from the eyrie of your eagle thought
Ye shall look down on monarchs."

A feeling of satisfaction with present attainments, a desire to relax in the efforts for improvement, is as fatal to the student as is sleep to the benighted traveller amid the snows of the Alps. Genius alone, if it be possessed, will be to us but as the hand of the sculptor, which is able indeed to form the beautiful statue from the shapeless block, but would never accomplish it while hanging listlessly by his side. Labor, untiring effort, must be the portion of every one who would accomplish anything great or good. We will not repine at it, but find in it our happiness. Let not the rust of inactivity consume our energies; let them be kept constantly bright with active and vigorous exercise. This is our business and pleasure in this life, and will it not be the same in the future? We may then rest from the labors of earth, but engage with untiring activity in those higher and nobler. "Mind is the perpetual motion. Sloth yields it not happiness; the bliss of a spirit is action."

IV.—Friendship and Love.

The young are often led by their impetuous natures into intimacies (I will not call them friendships) which are plainly unprofitable, in which one must feel herself contaminated by the gross faults or vices of another to whom she has professed, as she has felt, love. What shall be done in such a case? Shall the one who feels herself thus injured, for the fear of being called fickle, or the awakened malice of one she fears as an enemy, still wear the mask of friendship? Reason and conscience answer, No. Let such a friendship be broken off. But much caution is needed in such a case. If we deliberate before forming an attachment, it is no less important that we should do so before dissolving one. Are we sure there are sufficient reasons for such a step? Is it from some real fault of character that we wish to separate ourselves, or some ill feeling of our own for which we may be wholly to blame? If the necessity for breaking off an intimacy really exist, all care should be taken not to wound the feelings of the erring one unnecessarily, and on no account let any advantage gained over her by knowledge gained during the intercourse be used against her. Let all secrets be kept inviolate, all secret faults be never spoken. Be careful that hatred does not take the place of love. Always cherish a spirit of love and Christian forbearance to all. "Love your enemies." "Bless them that curse you." Be like Him who, when "He was reviled, reviled not again." Be not specially anxious to be loved. If you deserve it, you will find friends; if you love others, and discharge your duties to them humbly and faithfully, there will be some kindred spirits found whose natures will assimilate to your own, and with whom you may walk side by side in life's journey, cheering and cheered in the companionship. Be not forward in your professions of love. Nothing more surely defeats its object. If you have gained a friend, be grateful for him. Thank God for the blessing, than which none can scarcely be greater. If you feel that you have no friends, cast not the blame on others; seek within yourself the reason. If no one on earth speaks in friendship's tones, there is One above, ever in accents of love and mercy inviting us to his arms.

It speaks loudly in favor of the character of two individuals when they are seen preserving for a long time the character of friends. There are so many causes which may occur to interrupt transient intimacies. There is so much in the constant intercourse of two individuals calculated to try the temper, there are so many occasions calling for the spirit of forgiveness and self-denial, that the mere continuance of the connection speaks of many virtues of both parties.

While inculcating prudence in the choice of friends I would most earnestly warn you against the spirit of suspicion and censoriousness. Search for the good, believe you will find it as long as you can, and when you cannot, cast the mantle of charity over others' feelings. Treat no stranger in a manner inconsistent with the formation of a future friendship. The most repulsive at first sight may become your warmest friend. But restrain those expressions of warm love which you may feel till time has given some proof that the object of your adoration is a worthy one. By so doing you wrong no one; the bad and selfish receive their due; the good have the assurance that the love manifested is for the merit they have proved themselves to possess, and for which only they would be loved.

Love differs from friendship in degree, not in kind. Love is the perfection, the highest kind of friendship. Much of what is termed friendship is capricious: a kind of love being felt, and manifested on occasions, and the intervals perhaps filled up with indifference or dislike. But true friendship is uniform, a constantly pervading sentiment, seeking opportunities, it is true, of manifesting its strength, but never falling below a certain level. It does not consist in mere professions of regard, nor merely in kind looks or soft tones, but there is a spirit of self-sacrifice in behalf of the beloved one which is ever active. There is a willingness to conform to the wishes of another, to shape the conduct so as to please. There is a readiness to pardon faults. We ought none of us to be so unreasonable as to expect to find a friend in whom we can discover no fault, or as soon as we have learned the faults of an individual to conclude that we can never be friends. We know ourselves to be full of faults, and shall we refuse to others the indulgence we would claim for ourselves? Those who know us best will know the most of our failings and weaknesses: how necessary that they possess a forgiving spirit towards us. The proofs

of friendship are more in acts than words.
If a person will quietly, claiming nothing
of merit, sacrifice some anticipated pleasure or indulgence for my interest, if she
will show on all occasions a willingness to
oblige, if she is ever ready to lend a sympathizing ear to my tale of what deeply
interests me, if I am ever ready to do and
feel the same for her, if we can at the
same time feel that our souls are attuned
in unison, we may reasonably conclude
that we have proofs of friendship.

I cannot leave this subject without adverting to the provisions made for our
happiness by an all-beneficent Creator.
He has placed us amid trials for the
strengthening of our virtue; but he has
given us love for each other to irradiate
our path, else too full of darkness and
gloom. He places us amid endearing
family ties; he surrounds us with objects
on every hand to draw out our hearts in
love. We are always happy in loving.
There is enjoyment in our love of nature,
in our love for the brute creation, in our
love for members of our own family, in

our unutterable affection for a congenial spirit, in reverential adoration for our God! The jealousies, the envyings, the rivalries so often associated with love, form no more a part of it than did the persecutions of the Catholics in the Crusades form a part of the religion of Christ. The absence of love, the sudden ceasing of it, or the effort to cease, may cause sorrow and a "broken heart"; but never the exercise of love. It is a serious, a solemn thing to love. If we are allowed to love, let us thank our God that he has given us an object worthy of such love. We do not truly love unless we can make sacrifices for the object of that love. To quote a favorite author, "Love is a sweet idolater, enslaving all the soul, all the devotion of the heart, in all its depth and grandeur, a real living sacrifice to the God of all its worship."

Impulse or fancy too often are the sole directors of the young in forming the most important connections in life. Some act on the principle, "Love will go where it is sent," and often imagine it to be sent where a deformed and spurious substitute only is found. A deep, well-founded attachment is the only proper antecedent to marriage.

Our happiness consists in the gratification of our several faculties. Love is a blending together of these faculties in different individuals, a flowing together in harmony of thought and feeling; and the greater number of the faculties called into harmonious action, the greater will be the love. Thus we may love persons of very opposite characters. With one we may indulge in flights of fancy, enjoy the beautiful or the sublime; with another we may engage in argumentative discussions; and with another we may hold sweet converse on the things beyond the veil of sense. If our own natures have been properly cultivated and developed, if our minds are well balanced, we should not wish a companion for life who could sympathize with us in only one of these respects; but we should seek for a gratification of our whole nature, and the more perfect this agreement of natures the more perfect will be the love.

V. — THE STUDY OF NATURE.

Wherever we turn our eyes in this fair world in which we live we behold objects full of interest. The earth, air, and water teem with subjects for study, for long and close examination. Even a cursory view will awaken thoughts and call up feelings of no trifling values in the most ordinary breast. The wonders of creation have been noticed by all.

I was once much interested in hearing from my window a laboring man, of mean appearance, ask a clergyman who was observing his labors, why bitter and pleasant plants grew side by side, drawing their nourishment from the same soil? No answer was heard; and who can comprehend it? It is a mystery, and mysteries like this are on every side. We have but to open our eyes, and bend a listening ear, and thousands of such wonderful operations will be revealed to us. Who can explain the phenomena of the rising cloud and gathering tempest? Who can show the laws on which depend the changes of temperature, or regulate the course of the winds? Something may be learned, but who understands them fully? Who can explain the growth of vegetables, can show how the almost invisible organs are formed, and how they elaborate from the sap, so uniform in its appearance, the portion necessary to nourish a particular part of the plant? Who has seen the fairy wand, that, in the bowels of the earth, has, in thousands of rolling years, by almost imperceptible touches, formed the ruby or the sparkling diamond? Who can say that he has dived to the depths of any of nature's secrets? And is there not here room sufficient for the most ambitious student, a sphere of exercise wide enough for the most capacious powers?

The Baltimore oriole chooses the extremity of a limber twig, and there suspends its abode. I have seen one of these tiny habitations at the extremity of the waving branch of a lofty elm, where, moved by every breeze, it was secure from approach by the most hardy enemy of the bird race. It seemed to me sometimes to require powers of engineering equal to those of the most skilful gunner to enable the bird to enter her domicile during a violent wind.

The study of nature, in all its departments, expands the powers of the mind by constantly presenting the infinite and unfathomable. Dive as far as we may into the mysteries of nature, there is still an infinity beyond. Go on the wings of the imagination to the verge of the visible universe, you are only on the threshold of creation. Grasp as much as you can of her train of causes and effects, you find you have but touched the hem of their garments. Stretch the powers of your mind to the utmost to comprehend her operations, they fall back into themselves, wearied with the view of infinity. But these glimpses of the unsearchable incite the student of nature onward to make other and still other trials, and his "reward is with him." Never has he felt his toil unrepaid: he always finds a jewel, if not the very one he seeks. The study of nature has a remarkable power of soothing and calming the mind. When we have been learning that lesson which needs experience more than wisdom, that the world is full of guilt and misery, then we may go forth and breathe the fresh air, gaze upon the deep blue of the sky, feeling there is a world beyond, tread the verdant earth, hold converse with birds and flowers, and lo! the gloomy images have departed: we have received a heaven into our souls, where shines the light of truth and love. Who can indulge in angry and selfish passions when surrounded by the harmony of nature, with the pure eyes of holy angels reading the soul? Man comes forth from communion with such scenes better prepared for his duties to God and to his fellow, with more of the "milk of human kindness" to distribute around. Who can talk with the angels, even though they be of the brook or the flower, without his heart being made better? Genius may catch some of her loftiest inspirations from this converse with nature. Who that has a spark of the ethereal fire burning within him can look unmoved, with cold indifference, on her works? In whom will not the latent beam brighten into a flame, and by its effulgence cheer the path of other of earth's pilgrims, awakening perchance in them the power hidden in their breasts?

But higher than all this will the study of nature carry the true, the unperverted mind. Such must feel the need of a power to control so mighty operations, and with earnest adoration one will bow before a God. "An undevout astronomer is mad." An undevout observer of the putting forth of one tiny leaf, the budding and expansion of one delicate flower, is living in perversion of the highest powers of his nature. Who has fashioned the ribs of the earth? Who holds in appointed limits the rage of the swelling waters? Who tempers the air for man to breathe, and makes the animal creation observe their proper laws? From every nook of creation echoes the name of God! It is roared forth by the cataract, and whispered by the falling dew; it rumbles in the thunder, and rests in the gentle breeze; it is written on the broad firmament and on the petal of the lovely flower. All utter forth, God!

VI. — WOMANLY VIRTUE.

It would seem, perhaps, that the value of a virtuous character to a woman need not be commented on. But when we see the eagerness with which many run after the attractions of fashion and of accomplishments, the avidity with which they pursue the more solid branches of education even, without a thought for the moral nature, we may well inquire if their attention has ever been thoroughly aroused to this momentous subject. A young lady, in making her appearance into what is technically termed society, is usually the subject of much remark. She expects it, and she is supposed to have endeavored, with her friends' assistance, to so educate herself that she may be favorably received and esteemed. But how much of this anxiety has been expended, during her youthful days, upon the character of amiability, of benevolence, of true humble piety, which she shall bear? Not the manner in which she shall appear amiable and good, but that she shall really be so, should be the real cause of anxiety.

Virtue's garb may be worn, and often is, on special occasions, for limited periods, by those who can claim no affinity with the lawful owner. I shall speak on the importance of virtuous principles and habits to woman. What these principles are I need hardly pause to define. The example of Jesus of Nazareth and his teachings are before all. The obligations which they impose, to "deal justly, love mercy," "to love God and our neighbor," to regard our duties to him more than our friends, or even life itself, are well known. The moral law given by Moses, and our Lord's declaration, that "he came not to destroy this but to fulfil," should remove all doubt as to what is required of us as moral beings. Add to these the monitor within, which never sleeps unless by long and unceasing efforts to compel it to do so, and who can excuse herself for a want of knowledge of duty?

Such principles implanted in the heart keep from the disgrace and misery of open sin. I mean not those crimes against society and the laws of the land to which none of you have any temptation, but those exhibitions of evil temper and violent passions, of impatience and fretfulness and deception, which may have been seen darkening the fair brow and influencing the acts of the loveliest of the daughters of Eve. The display of such evil feelings must be considered a disgrace to any one, however she may have succeeded on special occasions in concealing them.

There is nothing which can give the friends of a young lady such pure delight as the thought that she is firmly intrenched in virtuous principles. Their fears for your safety, if such be your character, will never be called up, but rather a proud consciousness of your firmness in duty will rest in their minds. What a source of happiness to yourself to feel that your conduct is looked upon with satisfaction by those whom you honor and love. The happiness, too, of "a conscience void of offence" can be compared to no other. Truly, all we can do in way of self-denial is amply compensated; every act returns in blessing on our own head.

"As a man thinketh, so is he." No one can habitually indulge in foolish and trifling trains of thought, and at the same time be prepared to meet, with an equal mind, the trials and temptations of life. To say nothing of the sin against God of such thoughts, you may see the effect of them in action. The habit of indulging in dreams of the imagination, in "castle building," as it is called, is destructive to a high tone of moral feeling.

If you are endeavoring to form the character of a virtuous woman, you will be watchful of your conduct in private. Nothing will be done when concealed from every human eye which you would fear to have revealed. Little things should be done well. Little meannesses should be avoided. In your daily intercourse with those around you, with your schoolmates, teachers, and other friends, let the strictest honesty and fairness be preserved. Aim in all your dealings with them to obey the Golden Rule. Regard their rights in all things, whether they be present or absent. Avoid the unkind word or sly insinuation concerning the motives of

another. Avoid wounding the feelings
by allusions and otherwise. Do not wear
the appearance of taking no interest in
those with whom you daily meet, or
appear to conceal from some individuals
things which you reveal to others. Be
frank; be courteous; be really willing to
trouble yourself to oblige another. Great
exactions will not be made. Your kindness will not be presumed upon too far.
But in aiming thus to promote kind feeling and happiness, do not yield to temptations to do wrong, however alluring they
may be. Be firm in refusing to accom-
pany even your best friend, if she invites
you from the path of duty; and fear not
to reprove or express your disapproba-
tion when projects of which the justice is
questionable are proposed. Do not follow
a multitude to do evil. A regard for
the right will keep you clear of those
little differences and unpleasant feelings
towards each other which sometimes arise
among school girls. Of the folly of such
I will not speak. Suffice it to say that if
you feel right towards all a misunder-
standing cannot long exist. A consciousness of rectitude will enable you to go to

the estranged one, and together you can easily explain all, and I venture nothing in saying that in ninety-nine cases in a hundred you will find nothing as the foundation of all unkind feeling. If you have done wrong freely acknowledge it, and even if you cannot understand the motives of your companion, treat her still with honorable and Christian kindness.

All your intercourse with those whom you occasionally meet should be marked with a regard for the right. In all your dealings be firm and honorable. Let it be understood that you are not governed by caprice, but by fixed principles from which you cannot swerve. Do nothing which will risk your good name. Trifling acts in public places may be fatal to the reputation which you should all desire to possess. Let modesty and a regard for propriety distinguish you on all occasions.

The duties of loving and reverencing your parents should never be forgotten. A constant sense of their superior wisdom should be preserved. However greater than theirs your advantages have been for cultivating your minds, your obligations are the same, or even greater. It is sometimes the case, that young persons think themselves, on account of their superior education, free to despise the counsels and opinions of their elders; thus turning the weapon which those very parents have placed in their hands for a good purpose against them. A mind of the highest cultivation cannot, in its early development, have the benefit of that experience which forms the superiority of the more aged. Then, my dear young friends, use the best energies of your minds in promoting the welfare of those to whom you owe so much. Regard their wishes. Obey their every command. Show them that your cultivation of mind has refined your feelings and given you a delicacy in your treatment of them. Show that you are interested in all that concerns them. How many go abroad with sunshine on the countenance, but veil themselves in a cloud at home. How many spend time and talent in preparing to gain the applause of strangers, but by peevishness and ill-nature, give their best friends reason to despise them. Think of your parents as your best earthly friends. As said the Turkish prince, while mourning the loss of his mother, "Allah can give me many brothers and sisters and wives, but I can have but one mother." And he might have added, but one could ever love him as a mother. Truly might the parents of a virtuous daughter say: "Who can find such an one? Her price is far above rubies."

The rewards of the virtuous woman will be found in her own heart, in the consciousness of rectitude, of being the dispenser of joy around her. "It is more blessed to give than to receive." But the giver is blessed in giving and receiving. The kind words and deeds will return with interest to her who bestowed them. She has not, like the butterfly, fluttered in sunlight to attract the gaze of thoughtless idlers, or to amuse for the moment the more thoughtful, but, like the angel of mercy, she has gone forth to cheer and to bless the bowed down and the sorrowing. She passes through scenes of trial and temptation unscathed, and prepared for new proofs, like gold seven times purified. She lives not in vain dreams of Utopian happiness, but nerves herself to the duties of the present real world, and leaves it not as though she had never lived in it. Her mission ended, her duties all and well performed, she leaves this life like a "shock of corn fully ripe." Shall I attempt to look farther, and follow her beyond this world, and ask what are there her rewards? I must pause, "for eye hath not seen, nor ear heard" the joys of those who are at last found on the right hand of their Redeemer. We cannot realize the rapture with which she will strike the golden harp, or add her voice to those unceasing songs of praise. That you, my dear girls, may all be numbered with those who shall, in the world to which we are all hastening, wear the robe of Christ's righteousness, with His mark placed upon you, is the sincere and earnest prayer of her who addresses you.

FROM AN ADDRESS AT THE ORGANIZATION OF A BENEVOLENT SOCIETY.

We are benefited by everything that calls into exercise the highest faculties of our nature. Our whole enjoyment consists in the appropriate exercise of every function. Let any one of our powers lie dormant and a fountain of gratification is forever sealed. "The bliss of the spirit is action." "Happiness," says Dr. Johnson, "consists in the multiplication of agreeable consciousnesses." To be in the highest degree happy, to fulfil in the best manner the whole purpose of our being, our natures must be called into action: all our faculties must be engaged in harmonious exercise. The higher the rank of the faculties engaged, the greater the gratification of their action. There is a kind of satisfaction in revenge; how much higher that of Christian forgiveness! The pleasure derived from the sense of taste or smell may be great, but how much greater delight does the soul experience while drinking in beauty from the glowing evening sky, or from the outspread landscape of thousand hues and forms. All expansion and action of our higher powers elevates us in the scale of being, and is an increased capacity for happiness. Why should we doubt that it is " more blessed to give than to receive"? Why should we suppose that a good action benefits only the one for whom it is intended? And why should we congratulate the recipient of a favor, and envy not the one who possessed a heart noble and generous enough to devise the noble act? Is it because we fancy the possession of some tangible material substance the greatest of blessings? Who would not rather possess the heart of a Howard than all the dollars of an Astor? Affections are the coin of spirits; brutes may transport silver and gold. How much more desirable the spirit of an Ann H. Judson, — devoting to the miserable Burmans not one afternoon in a month, or one evening in a week by her pleasant fireside to labor for the heathen, but the loftiest energies of her noble soul, amid suffering and contumely, for her whole lifetime,—than all the homage which Queen Elizabeth, with three kingdoms at her feet, in her proudest moments, ever received? As the genius of the sculptor is more desirable than even the almost breathing image which his hand has made, as the soul of the poet in its high conceptions is even far above his most skilful embodiment of them, so is the heart which "devises liberal things" transcendently more blessed than the most favored receiver of them.

One self-denying, practical Christian, though her sphere be narrow, will accomplish more of real good than all the Owens and Fouriers the world has ever produced.

A benevolent act is like the sprouting of a seed in the soul; the smiles and tears of the recipient are the sunshine and showers which may bring the germ to maturity.

Our charities must begin at home and extend from it in every direction, so that our gratification may not be wholly of indigenous products, but consist in part of the luxuries of foreign climes. In a thousand forms there comes to the soul the reward of disinterested benevolence.

"Every flower on other's pathway strown,
 Reflects its fragrant beauty on our own."

It is strange that the temptation is not stronger than it seems to be, to be benevolent from selfishness. A refined kind of selfishness it would indeed be, conceiving it in any sense proper to call by such a name the pleasure resulting from a purely benevolent act.

A man is never in a better condition to praise God than when he has been extending the hand of charity to one of his creatures. It is difficult to see how a man can love Jesus Christ and not love those for whom he died. That he does not is a strong argument against his piety.

Our faculties act in clusters. Love to God, love to man, love to all the creatures of God, love to every atom and every system of worlds that he has made, flow forth alike from the heart in unison with his requirements.

> "He prayeth well, who loveth well
> Both man and bird and beast."

How glorious the thought that in doing good we are co-workers with God! That he condescends to style us fellow laborers with him! That in so doing we are becoming more like him into whose image we hope to be transformed! We may reflect, too, with satisfaction on the good accomplished through our humble instrumentality. We may follow in imagination our gifts to their destination. We may fancy the sparkling eye, the glad smile, and the joyous tones of those enjoying our bounty. We may fancy the heart of the missionary on distant shores blessing the means of renewed usefulness we have given him. We may, by a loftier flight of imagination, catch from the spirit world the song of redeeming love taught some heathen soul from the word of life we once sent to him.

FROM A LECTURE ON ART EDUCATION.

There are to be found in the present day numerous circles where art and art productions are discussed *ad nauseam*; from which a casual visitor, possessed of some knowledge of art and with a reverence for it, retires, disgusted for the moment with the whole subject. But this same visitor has more often encountered the opposite extreme; he has fallen among people entirely ignorant of artistic matters.

either supposing themselves competent to pronounce judgment upon any and every work of art, or, confessing their ignorance, glorying in it, and professing to despise the whole race of artists and their productions. I think, however, that we find, especially since the "Centennial," more reasonable views of the subject and a greater desire to be informed concerning it than formerly. But the indifference is still deplorable. I once invited some recent graduates of a theological seminary, who had lived three years within half an hour of a great city without discovering the locations of its art galleries, to look at a collection of engravings, Doré's Tennyson and Retsch's Outlines being among its attractions. They excused themselves for want of time. (It was their vacation at the end of their professional course, you remember.) A venerable gentleman, who had been president of three or four colleges, after listening to a lecture to undergraduates, in which the manner of producing the different styles of engravings was explained, confessed that he had never before in his life thought of the subject.

I knew of a father whose son had shown some skill in the art of drawing, and who desired to learn more of it, objecting to the request on the ground that it would make the boy, as he said, "namby-pamby." We remember that the father of Frederick the Great forbade his flute playing for a similar reason, and we can understand how the half-savage old Prussian king felt in the matter: but it is not so easy to comprehend why a man desiring a peaceful career for his son in this nineteenth century should fear the influence of artistic instruction. In those times, when might made right, when war offered the only chance to win distinction, the peaceful pursuits of the man of science or of the artist might naturally be regarded with distrust; but in this good time which has come such distrust shows but a mistaken idea of the nature and objects of art. That it is not necessarily demoralizing or enervating may be shown by reference to artists who have led noble and manly lives, and who have stood strong and good among the strongest and best. The names of Michael Angelo, Sir Joshua Reynolds, and Benjamin West of former times, and of our own Powers, Story, and Harriet Hosmer of to-day, will occur to all.

I purpose speaking to you on the subject of art as a branch of liberal education. I purpose to inquire what art may do for a man or a woman who does not pursue it as a profession, and who even may produce no works of art at all.

Art may be defined (in the words of another) as "the pursuit of beauty and of truth, or that continued attempt to express and multiply ideas of truth and beauty which seems to be natural to all well-developed races of men." The arts of painting and sculpture, by means of lines and colors, produce ideas of truth and beauty. Music, poetry, and eloquence are reckoned among the fine arts, and they present ideas which are invested with what may be called beauty by analogy. The term beauty may be applied to anything which is well developed, complete, or excellent in its kind. "As for the nature of beauty," says Mr. Ruskin, "it seems to defy all real analysis; and this, and its universal presence, and the intensely powerful feeling it awakens, seem to point to its being a direct manifestation of Divine Power."

The principles of art may be studied to advantage by all, and best studied by giving some attention to its practice. "If ye will do, ye shall know of the doctrine," is as applicable in this as in moral actions.

*

The question of power to learn to draw rightly is simply one of a little time and a little earnest attention. The idea that a hand and eye that can thread a needle and work a button-hole, that can strike a nail on the head or bring down a bird on the wing, cannot draw any form that is really attempted by their owner is absurd. The same faculties that are used in forming the letters of the alphabet in writing are all that are needed in drawing correctly.

*

The first exercise of the mind, when any knowledge is to be acquired, is that of attention. It is the first thing to be secured in the training of any living thing, be it animal or child. And often the difference between two minds, one of which is capable of grasping and retaining all that is presented to it, and the other unable to succeed in any attempt however small, is, that in the first there is the power of fixed attention which the second lacks. Now in drawing, from copies or from nature, the attention must be held to its object. The attention once fixed, a thousand things before unseen come out and range themselves before the eye. Differences appear which the untrained and careless eye never saw. A new power of observation is gained which stimulates to renewed effort, and often the eye, which began by seeking only for form and color, beholds correspondence of parts, analogies and uses, and the student of art finds himself in the pursuit of science without losing his devotion to the fairer sister whom first he wooed. Audubon, the distinguished American ornithologist, began to study birds with a view only to the representation of their plumage by painting. His interest in the beautiful objects he depicted, growing by what it fed upon, led him on to those extended observations into the habits of the feathered creation, which have enriched science for all time, and placed Audubon's name among those of the first naturalists of the world.

It is interesting to observe, that, in our own and other languages, the word expressive of moral correctness and that for the shortest distance between two points is the same. A right line, a right action, *rectum; rectus*, right, straight. A pupil who is learning to draw has his mind constantly occupied with ideas of right. Accuracy, correctness, precision, must characterize the work of every moment. Is it possible that a love of truth can fail to be promoted by this daily and hourly association with her? And may not some appreciation of the beauty of moral rectitude be thus indirectly acquired? There may be bad men who are good artists, as there are no doubt undevout astronomers who are not mad; but I cannot conceive of a devotee of truth in art, who is wholly insensible to her influence in morals.

There is an important part of our nature which is peculiarly developed by the study of art. Our faculty of observation, our power of attention, our reasoning and critical powers, our general intelligence, may all be stimulated and improved, perhaps, by other studies as well as by this, but our æsthetic nature, all that part of our being which discovers and enjoys beauty in its varied forms, is especially called into action by art study. It is the æsthetic faculty which responds to the harmony of sweet sounds; which swells with rapture as the images of the poet or of the orator float before the mind; which kindles with enthusiasm at the sight of the resplendent sky or glowing landscape; which pants with longing for the infinite as the eye rests on the boundless expanse of the ocean; or which seeks to penetrate the heavens in the blue distances where the mountains, peak behind peak, recede until they are lost to our view in a remote mystery which forbids our further search. It is this which enjoys beauty in all its aspects; which delights in the graceful outlines and harmonious coloring of all common objects; which finds pleasure amid toil, while beholding the well proportioned utensil or neatly fashioned tool which must be used for common or mean purposes; which rejoices in the creation of graceful forms, and which, when once awakened, can never sleep, but will continue to give a sense of enjoyment of beautiful things throughout life. It is this part of our constitution which, at this time, and with us in America, is most in danger of lying dormant. Everything seems adverse to its cultivation. The Anglo-Saxons, as a race, are in the greatest danger of neglecting it, while they have the greatest need of its influence. To use one of Lowell's "*sesquipedalia verba*," we need to be "desaxonized." The Latin races, with their love of sensuous delights, with their eager, passionate natures, may be drawn away from serious and earnest pursuits by a too great devotion to art; and it is these nations that have, in the cultivation of a debasing and enervating art, marked the era of their decline by the climax of their attainments in it. But the Anglo-Saxon is practical, easily absorbed in business and material concerns, is rough and stern, and prone to despise the gentler influences of an advanced civilization, greatly as they are needed for his completeness of character. Schiller, in the " Song of the Bell," speaking of the combination of metals needed for a perfect toned bell, says, —

"Where the strong is betrothed to the weak,
  And the stern in sweet marriage is blent with
    the meek.
  Rings the concord harmonious."

But few people are aware of the influence of education over our power of seeing. The enjoyment of natural beauty is greatly heightened, and seems in some instances to have been actually created, by a knowledge of the principles of art, by a love of pictures, and the habit of studying them. And there is nothing like actual drawing to enable one to see the beauties of a picture, or to discover beauty in natural objects. Draw common things, and you will see in them what the poet sees in them; you will look at them with something of the sense of beauty with which artists behold them. Beauty may be in the soul of the beholder, but the eye must be taught and encouraged to recognize it, and there is nothing better to teach one to see a thing than the attempt to portray it. Very slight success in such an attempt gives very great pleasure, although in the pursuit be the reward to be sought rather than the result.

Works of Art. — Regard these works as we may, we cannot refuse to believe that there is something in them worth looking for. We cannot imagine that sensible men have lived and worked their lives into these pictures and statues and monuments, and that there is nothing in them after all. The art student learns the language which the artist uses; he learns the symbols by which his ideas are expressed, and how to gather as from a new world ideas and impressions which could never have found expression in words, — which through the medium of art alone can find expression. And when we think of the many men throughout the ages who have thus lived and wrought their souls into their works, men God-endowed with genius, whose flight no obstacles could hinder, when we think of them and the legacies they have left to mankind, shall we dare to conclude that we can reap no benefit from their heaven-inspired endeavors, that it is not worth our while to attempt to look into the world in which they lived, and that the realm of wood and iron, of mathematics and steam, is all that we desire to know. It is true we may not have the opportunities we would wish to observe great works, but we may improve such as we have, and we may, by reading what has been written on art, learn how to improve them.

Aside from the knowledge of art we may derive from works on art subjects, there is often much else that is valuable. A highly intelligent lady writes to me recently, "I have never found better doctrine inculcated in any class of works than in art writings. Tyrwhitt and Ruskin seem to me to be imbued with a kindred spirit of love and purity and philanthropy."

In whatever way we may gain it, it is no small thing to have gained the power of earnest admiration of something out of ourselves. The spirit even which is ascribed to sentimental young ladies, and with them finds expression in many an "oh! ah! splendid! or mag!" is less to be deprecated than the morose, unappreciative disposition of the man who never sees excellence anywhere, and who, like Iago, "is nothing if not critical." Admiration of nature or of works of art is entirely unselfish, and is one of the highest forms of human pleasure. It is worth something to have the power of forgetting ourselves, especially when this forgetfulness involves a delighted recognition of something superior to ourselves.

To the amateur, art is a recreation, and takes the place to him that the daily newspaper, the gossiping neighbor, or the place of public entertainment, occupies with others. The desultory attention which such persons devote to their work does little more than enable them to furnish amusement for themselves and their friends, yet much may be said in favor of amusement so cheap, simple, and elevating. And although the æsthetic faculty and the moral sense must be regarded as distinct, and the development of the idea of beauty by no means involves that of conscience, the practice of amateur art may, while elevating the taste, at the same time keep the young from debasing amusements or the paths of vice. But let the amateur be condemned to hours and days of tedious leisure, to prolonged waiting for any cause, let him be subject to invalidism which destroys not the powers of hand and eye, and he is found to possess a resource which may save him from irritation, from insanity, idiocy, or from beggary. The productions of amateurs often call forth as great admiration as those of the great master of painting. It has been said that there never was a picture but pleased somebody. While the taste of the amateur himself may be so constantly progressing as to keep him dissatisfied with his work, yet he experiences a pleasure in his efforts, and he can always find those who may be benefited to the full extent to which a work of art is capable of contributing to their improvement, on whom the bestowal of his productions will be the greatest of favors. No gifts are more prized by the wealthy and cultivated than those which the hand of the giver has wrought. Thus may the spirit of kindness and benevolence, of love and friendship, be delightfully exercised in connection with the practice of only amateur art.

All the decorative arts are employed in the production of beauty, and we are so made that we enjoy beautiful forms in the pattern of a wall paper or of a carpet, in the form of a water pitcher or of a chair, as truly as in a painted Madonna or a sculptured Venus. The sense of beauty once thoroughly awakened, and properly directed by judicious culture, uncouth forms, gaudy colorings, and tinsel decorations will cease to appear in our daily surroundings. The dress of the human beings around us will become a more fitting and beautiful adornment of a temple illumed by the Shekinah of a human soul; our cities, our towns, and our villages will present groupings and colors which we can look upon without a shudder; our public buildings will adorn our native soil, making us love it yet more and more; our churches, instead of suggesting the dwellings of felons or of fiends, will, with their surroundings, look like the abodes of peace, and be indeed pleasant places in which the weary and thirsting soul may find the rest and refreshment which it seeks.

A taste for the beauty of natural scenery seems to be usually developed late in the life of nations and of individuals. The early painters did not represent it, the early poets have not sung of it. General literature, previous to the last hundred years, contains but few enthusiastic descriptions of scenery. The country, among all but modern writers, was looked upon as the place where beef and mutton were fattened, and where fruit and vegetables grew. Two or three proverbial sayings, quoted by a recent English writer, will tolerably well express all we know concerning the feeling of those men about scenery. One is the mythic Frenchman's, "*Aimez vous les beautés de la Nature? Pour moi, je les abhorre!*" Another comes from an Englishman, "I find Nature abominably in my way!" And a third is the ironical question and answer of Christopher North, "What is the motive with which a thinking man should undertake a journey to the Lakes? Why, the eating and drinking, to be sure!" I think if we could investigate the experience of most men and women who are now ardent lovers of scenery, we should find in the great majority of cases that the sensibility to its influence was developed after childhood, if not somewhat late in life, and that this development was not spontaneous, but the result of some influence from without; that the contagion of some friend's enthusiasm, or more probably the sight of finely painted landscapes, first awakened the interest which ripened into admiration. All this, I need not say, points to the importance of art education, and illustrates its civilizing and ennobling effects.

What, after all, do we get from pictures, from scenery and from art, that we should care to gain, and which will repay us for all this attention and labor?

Suppose you find beauty, what then? I will resort to Robert Browning and reply:

"If you get simple beauty and naught else,
You get about the best thing God invents,—
That's somewhat. And you'll find the soul you've
 missed,
Within yourself when you return him thanks."

You will find:

"The beauty and the wonder and the power,
The shapes of things, their colors, lights and
 shades,
Changes, surprises,— and, God made it all!

"What's it all about?
To be passed over, despised, or dwelt upon,
Wondered at? This world's no blot for us,
Nor blank,— it means intensely, and means good."

Education in itself often seems to me a very wonderful thing, or, rather, perhaps I should say that it seems wonderful that we are made capable of being educated. Why were we not made as the animals and plants, with a fixed and determined nature which should develop under all circumstances with very nearly the same characters and aspects? For although many animals may be trained or educated, training and education mean very different things with them and with us. Why is it that we regard an infant, fresh from the hand of its Maker, as a less perfect being than the old man who has passed through the conflicts of life, and who has become educated in intellect and in character? Why is it that the circumstances of birth and education are allowed to place their stamp upon the human soul, so that, in all outward characteristics, the man born and living in Turkey is essentially a different being from an Esquimaux or an Englishman? And taking another view of the matter, how strange is it that we may ourselves choose the die which shall leave its impress upon us, that we may determine for ourselves the direction in which our faculties shall grow, that we may decide the form and stature which we shall attain? How incomprehensible is that arrangement by which in our greatest immaturity and weakness we must decide upon paths whose terminations we cannot see, but which differ from each other as light from darkness! But the responsibility laid upon us should make us careful and earnest, and eager to seize on all the helps which may be in our way; it should lead us to accept in our blindness the sure and infallible guide which Providence and " the Word" furnish. The wise heart will find wisdom, and all may be secured which is needed to make us perfect men and women, nothing left out and nothing out of proportion.

※

Education should be symmetrical. All our powers were given us for use, and all need their appropriate culture. "As the eye cannot say to the hand, nor the hand to the foot, I have no need of you," so cannot the reason say to the imagination, or the imagination to the fancy, "I require you not." No one of the ten talents was bestowed to be laid up in idleness. Like the many keys of the piano, all of which may not be needed in every piece of music performed, and which yet must be in their place and kept in tune, the faculties of the human soul are all given for some good purpose, and should all be held in that condition most favorable for their action. They should "stand and wait" that their service may be rendered when required. Every stone is as necessary to the perfection of the arch as the keystone. And although, in the Corinthian temple, every pillar may not be necessary to the support of the cornice and architrave, all are requisite for its symmetry and beauty, and no one is so insignificant as not to be missed by the Master who has planned the structure, and to whom the builders must render an account of their work.

FROM A LECTURE ON **ENGRAVING**.

It is one of the blessings of our present age that works of art are scattered everywhere among the people. This distribution illustrates in a striking manner the tendencies of ancient and modern institutions. Formerly all works of art were confined to the wealthy and privileged classes. Now every laborer's cottage and every factory girl's room may contain engravings and perhaps vases and statuettes as beautiful, if not as costly in material, as those which formerly graced the royal palace. I am sure you will thank me if I here quote from Mr. Ruskin, who expresses what I would say so much better than I could hope to do: "The great lesson of history is that all the fine arts as practised hitherto have only accelerated the ruin of the states they advanced; and at the moment when, in any kingdom, you point to the triumphs of its greatest artists, you point also to the determined hour of the kingdom's decline. The names of great painters are like passing bells: in the name of Velasquez, you have sounded the fall of Spain; in the name of Titian, that of Venice: in the name of Leonardo, that of Milan; in the name of Raphael, that of Rome. And there is profound justice in this, for hitherto, the greater the art, the more surely has it been used, and used solely, for the decoration of pride,— whether religious or profane pride, is no matter,— or the provoking of sensuality. Another course lies open to us. For us there can be no more the throne of marble, for us no more the vault of gold, — but for us there is the loftier and lovelier privilege of bringing the power and charm of art within the reach of the humble and the poor; and as the magnificence of past ages failed by its narrowness and its pride, ours may prevail and continue by its universality and its lowliness."

We have pictures everywhere, in our school books, in our newspapers, on our walls, and we may make collections in scrap-books and portfolios which will be a source of enjoyment to us when fatigued or ill, or may help to cheer the weary invalid when other sources of pleasure have all failed. And we may have opportunities of seeing collections of paintings, as we visit the city, where one may always find free exhibitions of fine works, or for a small fee may see choice or rare pictures. The Art Museum in Boston is free to all on Saturdays, with all its treasures of antiques, of sculptures, and of casts from works which no money could buy, and which only a voyage across the Atlantic and much weary journeying could enable us to see in the originals. The paintings and engravings at the Museum cannot fail to interest all, and if one has but an hour to spend would well repay the effort of a visit. Just as a show, the Art Museum is more attractive than hundreds of the cheap shows for which so many are willing to pay their money.

All painting, engraving, or art generally, is but a language by which thoughts or feeling may be expressed. One may learn to make pictures just as one may learn to write, to form words and sentences, and to arrange them grammatically, without expressing any valuable thought. We should not value as a literary work a volume of beautifully written or printed pages in which only finely executed letters and a harmonious jingle of sounds were to be found. We value what is written more than we do the manner of saying it, and nonsense is nonsense however elaborately expressed. So the coarsest lithograph or wood-cut may be precious to us if it brings us into sympathy with a beautiful scene or beautiful thought. I am not saying that the manner of expressing anything in either literature or art (or manners in any sense) is of no importance, but only that we must look beyond the mode of expression for the highest merit. In selecting pictures, select those that mean something to you, that soothe you by their quiet beauty, elevate you by their grandeur, or inspire you by their heroism. Your taste will change in regard to pictures, as with poetry and everything else, but you will never despise a former object of admiration if it were sincerely chosen for something it really said to you. Learn something of art; it will not hinder your work or your business. Take this, too, along with you in the journey of life. Look at pictures; look at all beautiful objects. Learn all you can about them; learn to look to nature for that which the painter saw and represented. Look for beauty in nature; if you find it, it will not interfere with the other things which you find. You can study stones and flowers and bugs just as well while enjoying the landscape in which you find them, or the bright hues which they themselves reveal.

There is a story of a prince on whom a

variety of gifts was lavished at his birth. Last of all, his uncle, an enchanter, bestowed on him the power of seeing the fairies. "He shall see all the hidden beauty and latent life which other men's eyes are not fine enough to see. He shall know the fretful spirits that live under the holly leaves and in the curls of the young ferns: and beneath the scarlet mushrooms: and on the stones of the field all scarlet and green: and in the orange and gray lichens of old oak roots. He shall know all about the dwellers in the Alpine rose, and meet face to face 'the brown men of the moors that stay beneath the heather bell.' He shall understand the life that is in the leaves, and how they faint under the heat of noon, and drink deep of summer rain. He shall know the spirits of structure and growth, and the toughness of old yews and thorns, and the sad strength of the fir and cypress. He shall also be on terms with the spirits of fire and light, and the living rays that make color of sky and cloud and distance: and with all underground tribes who stain earths and metals and jewels, and dole out the elements of man's frame with all its beauty and its fearfulness and wonder,— seeing to this day it is made of the substance of the earth and dust of the ground. And having all these gifts he will care little for what vulgar men strive for, and nothing for what evil men desire; and the common troubles of life will touch him lightly, for he will have that within him which they cannot touch. And because of the friends he sees and who see him, he shall always bear himself gently and stoutly among men, with an high heart and an humble spirit." " Something like this gift to the fairy prince is that of having one's eyes open to the beauty of common things. In any case, every possible means of refinement, and every possible access to harmless enjoyment, and every possible encouragement to the sense of beauty," is the thing most needful to us all in this age of material and mercenary tendencies.

There is a tendency with some persons to undervalue engravings and pictures. "Only a picture," is all some people will say of any representation of external nature that can be shown them. An artist once made a very fine painting of an animal belonging to the herd of a farmer, which picture, when completed, was valued at some hundreds of dollars. When shown to the owner of the herd he expressed great surprise at the price of the picture, and exclaimed, "Why, you could have half my cattle for that money!" A painting of a ruined cottage or of a broken down mill, with its disabled water wheel, has often been sold for a price that the objects at their best would never have commanded. These things only go to show that the world sets a value on pictures, even if some of us fail to see it. The picture brings to our notice things we never saw or cared to see in nature, and often interests the beholder in looking at nature to verify the picture, and so helps to create a habit of observation which may be a source of great pleasure. A good picture represents not only the objects painted, but the emotions that the view of beautiful objects produce in the mind of the painter, which will be high and noble according to the genius of the man. The painter of genius adds to his work "the gleam, the light that never was on sea or land, the consecration, and the poet's dream."

"For, don't you mark, we're made so that we love
  First when we see them painted, things we have
    passed
  Perhaps a hundred times nor cared to see;
  And so they are better, painted—better to us,
  Which is the same thing. Art was given for
    that—
  God uses us to help each other so,
  Lending our minds out."
            ["Fra Lippo Lippi." Browning.]

FROM A LECTURE ON CATHEDRALS.

THE thousands of statues on the outside of the cathedral of Milan are all in white marble, like the edifice itself. They are placed on the top of spires and pinnacles, in little recesses of the Gothic tracery, in groups, on façades, and at the base of the pointed arches. The parts of the cathedral, with the statues, near the ground are clouded with yellowish brown stains, but the nearer the spires, with their accompanying angels, approach the sky, the whiter and purer do they appear. Perhaps from this fact of the exterior, one of the best lessons of the cathedral may be learned. Nothing can be more beautiful than these heaven-kissing pinnacles in the light of the morning or evening sun. The general form of the building may not be wholly satisfactory, it looks rather flat and broad, but the richness of the sculptures and the beauty of the coloring cannot be surpassed. I am reminded here of our courier, who, when we asked him from time to time if the cathedrals we were anticipating were finer than those we had already seen, would invariably reply, "Quite a different thing, missis." Cologne, Strasbourg, and Milan, the three great Gothic cathedrals of Europe, can by no means be compared. Cologne, gray in color, vast and massive, is not at all like Strasbourg, dark in color, but rising, as if at a bound, untrammelled by gravitation, a structure of stony lace, held in place by some mysterious power, and liable to be overthrown by the next breeze! Then Milan, white, solid, a crystallization rather than a structure, on which the spirits of the air have alighted, to be forever fixed by some strange enchantment.

What do these structures accomplish? As far as they are specimens of high and noble art they gratify our taste for the beautiful, they meet the cravings of the æsthetic part of our nature. But emotions of taste are not identical with religious emotions. The idea of breathing is not the idea of sight; the emotion of grandeur is not the emotion of worship. If the art be truly pure and noble, it will elevate the soul and fit it, perhaps, for a better class of emotions than those it can itself give. But we have only to observe the character of those people who are most highly favored with specimens of what we call religious art, to be convinced that it does but little towards renewing and elevating the character. Yet we cannot deny that external things have their influence upon our feelings, and architectural forms may symbolize to us high and noble aspirations, and aid our souls in mounting upward. Nature certainly does this, as we all have felt, and she comes to us with grand and beautiful aspects which art may vainly try to excel. If costly works of art are an aid to religion, then those who cannot possess them or visit them are deprived of a great and important means of culture. We may regret our inability to enjoy them to the extent we might wish, but we all may seek the inspiring influences of nature. We may look on the beautiful frost work of winter, on the crystal palaces in the wintry woods,— we may admire the beautiful flowers of spring, and lie on the summer grass to gaze through the Gothic arches of lofty living forest trees, — we may raise our eyes to the vast dome of the sky, with its panorama of clouds by day and stars by night, — we may forget the splendors of colored glass when we behold the rainbow spanning the heavens, or gaze as it were into the open doors of heaven itself in the morning or evening sky, — we may send our thoughts upward, as our eye climbs up to the top of Alpine peaks, thousands of feet above us, — and, as we behold the illimitable prairie, the sky touching lake, or the boundless ocean,— vastness and infinity may call forth the longings of our soul. All these we may enjoy if our eyes are open to see their glories, while we remember, too, that there is another Mediator with God than these external forms, who has said, "The hour cometh, when ye shall neither in this mountain, nor yet at Jerusalem, worship the Father," and who has often fulfilled his promise of blessing to his disciples by meeting with the humblest of his children in the lowliest of hovels.

FROM A LECTURE ON MICHAEL ANGELO.

I once met in the work of a brilliant writer this remark: "There are four men in the world of art and of literature exalted above all others, and to such a degree as to seem to belong to another race, namely, Dante, Shakespeare, Beethoven, and Michael Angelo." It seems to me that the last named of these, though equally, at least, with the first three worthy to be known and honored, is really but little known or appreciated by those whose honor and appreciation are the just tribute to great men. The reason may lie in the character of his works. We seldom admire what we have never seen, and while we dwell with delight upon the pages of Dante and Shakespeare, or listen with rapture to the strains of Beethoven, and feel that our souls are in communication with these master spirits, Michael Angelo seems far away from us, like a being of another age or another sphere of existence. His works, if we may behold them, are many of them dimmed by age, and we never regard copies, however good, with the same interest we feel in the original, genuine work of the artist's hand, nor do we feel that we can in them see the man himself, as we believe we do in reading the written page of an author, or in listening to the most ordinary rendering of a musical composition.

There is a tendency, too, to undervalue the whole race of artists, especially painters and sculptors, makers of pictures and "stone images." We scarcely imagine them men and Christians, possessed of noble or heroic qualities. We are so "buried in the waters of the actual" that those who minister only to our æsthetic nature, who only create something pretty for us to look at, are regarded as necessarily frivolous and useless beings, if not actually pernicious to society in leading people from the proper business of life. We can only come out of these illusions by learning that facts are against us, which we may do by studying the lives of these people and learning what they really are.

No one can contemplate the life of Michael Angelo Buonarotti without respect and admiration, and a reverence amounting almost to veneration. He is, like one of his own statues, many sided, and worthy of being viewed from every point. He was painter, sculptor, architect, and poet. He was, too, a true man and a Christian. His character in its loftiness and purity of aim, in its energy and devotion to duty, would interest us had he been possessed of only ordinary talent and capacity. As a man of genius he is worthy of our admiration and most careful study.

Few works of art have called out more enthusiasm than his famous statue of Moses. It was in the workshop forty years. It has been called the crown of modern sculpture, and both in idea and execution is incomparable. It has been said that Michael Angelo here embodied both himself and Julius. The power which the artist felt in himself is exhibited in the limbs and frame, and the demon-like, passionate vehemence of the Pope is seen in the countenance. Photographs of this statue are common, and there are casts in this country. No cast, however, can do justice to a marble statue. Plaster poorly takes the place of the delicate, transparent marble, which almost seems possessed of a calm, contemplative life.

※

Morning and Evening, Night and Day. — these, with the statutes of Lorenzo and Guliano de Medici, form two of the finest groups of statuary in the world. Grimm says: "The two dukes opposite to each other present the contrast of brooding reflection, and of resolve, rising into action. Guliano sits like a general on the summit of a hill looking down on his fighting soldiers. Lorenzo, deaf to all about him, seems lost in inward contemplation." We must remember that critics are divided as to the identity of these statues. Mr. C. C. Perkins considers the figure just described, and sometimes found as a bronze ornament under the name of "Contemplation," to be Lorenzo, while Grimm plainly designated this as Guliano. The design of the figures, reclining on sarcophagi at the feet of these dukes, seems to be to represent time symbolically; those at the feet of Guliano present the perfect contrast between life and death. Night, a female figure, "La Notte," in profound repose, symbolizes the powerlessness of death; Day, a powerful male figure, "Il Giorno," just awaking to perfect activity, is a symbol of the resurrection from the dead. "The Evening Twilight and Early Dawn," at the foot of Lorenzo, represent the passage of the soul from one state to the other. The manly figure, "Il Crepuscolo," is sinking into rest; the female "L'Aurora," just casting off her slumber, is awaking to immortality. These statues have called forth the utmost enthusiasm of critics. They are compared with the best specimens of Greek art, and believed by many to rival them. Of the six figures, that of Giuliano is the only one completely finished. Angelo generally worked up the face last; that of Lorenzo only wants the finishing touches. The faces of the four statues on the sarcophagi are all — I use Angelo's favorite figure — more or less veiled by the unremoved marble. The limbs, too, have not been wholly extricated; the figures seem struggling forth from the stone. This may be the best place to remind you of the verses of

Michael Angelo addressed to Vittoria Colonna, founded on his idea of the statue in the block.

"As when, O lady mine! with chiselled touch,
    The stone, unhewn and cold,
    Becomes a living mould,
The more the marble wastes, the more the statue grows:
So, if the working in my soul be such
That good is but evolved by time's dread blows,
    The vile shell, day by day,
    Falls like superfluous flesh away.
Oh! take whatever bonds my spirit knows,
And reason, virtue, power, within me lay!"

Is art worthy our time and attention? Such a question will be answered by considering that God must have had a purpose when he created men to produce artistic works, and made mankind generally to feel a need of them and a satisfaction in them. He created beauty as truly as the material for food and clothing. He might have made the world without flowers, without stars, without music, and yet to bring forth fruits, to be visible in the light, and vocal with speech. Why he has not done so we may not wholly know. Men possess in greater or less degree creative power, than which nothing more truly exalts them and allies them with God himself. All men, even children, delight in making something, be it a toy, a machine, or a work of art. The creative power of genius is possessed by few, but those few stand out in the history of the world as gods and heroes whom posterity will not willingly let die. But while there are few great artists, there are many capable in some degree of enjoying and appreciating art. Gœthe said, "Thou resemblest whom thou comprehendest." In comprehending the works of a great master, we are ennobled in our own esteem, and really elevated to a higher plane of existence. Thus, that cannot be an unimportant part of our nature which delights in beautiful things, in the beauties not only of nature but of art, and that it is a legitimate hunger which can only be gratified by the grand and the beautiful, as truly as that which seeks nourishment for the body, is attested by such noble lives as the one we contemplate in this lecture.

Questions are often raised as to the influence of works of art upon the moral nature. No decisive answer can be given. Milton leads his hosts of rebel angels to

> "the Dorian mood
> Of flutes and soft recorders,"

as they proceed to the erection of the "Doric pillar overlaid with golden architrave" in Pandemonium; and the songs of the redeemed and their golden harps resounding amid the arches of heaven are among the most familiar images. Art may render attractive the paths of vice, as well as decorate the straight and rugged way of virtue. It is an instrument to be used in the service of heaven or of hell. The same work may be to one beholder an angel of love and purity, and to another it may suggest only what is debasing and devilish. The question, too, is often discussed whether the emotions raised by painting, sculpture, architecture, and music are as intense as those called up by the writings of the poet, — a question which it is idle to discuss as it is not possible to weigh and measure the emotions of a single breast, much less those of mankind at large.

Works of art have a language which speaks to the soul capable of reading it as truly as the printed page, but the knowledge of different languages is not universal nor innate, and as little may we expect some men to understand the sentiment of a picture or of a statue, as that of a poem written in a tongue which they have never learned.

The world is full of beauty, but the beauties of nature do not satisfy the civilized man, and he early seeks to create for himself that which, suggested by nature, is yet not nature. He places the picture in his dwelling, the statue in the public square, and plants on the beloved soil of his native land those monuments and lofty piles which his love for it has dictated, and which placed there make it more dear. And, in our anticipation of the Celestial City, I think it cannot be irreverent to imagine the pearly gates beautiful in form and proportion as in material, and the towers and palaces in contour and workmanship worthy of the foundation of precious stones and the golden streets among which they rise.

FROM A LECTURE ON **WINDS AND WAVES.**

I HAVE given you a limited and very imperfect view of one class of the phenomena of our globe. I have brought you but a breath from the domain of the air, but a drop from the realm of the ocean. The phenomena we have been considering are but a link in the great chain of causes and effects which make up the great system of nature. But they are sublime in their very connections, reaching to the sun and moon and starry heavens on the one hand, and to the microscopic organisms of darkness and the deep on the other. We cannot give a glance like this of to-day towards the machinery of nature without an enlarged conception of the Creator's works, and the extent of the field of scientific research. We have in our subject an illustration of the practical value of science. The mariner can to-day, by taking advantage of the winds and currents, whose direction has been marked out for him, sail directly upon the most favorable routes from one quarter of the globe to another, when in former times, " the pathways of the deep" unknown, "the wind in his circuits" a mystery, he might lie for months rotting and starving, without a breeze to waft him on his way; or wandering into the region of the furious typhoons or the whirling cyclones might be lost amid storms and tempests. But setting aside all practical considerations, it ought to be sufficient for us to know that in studying the world which Supreme Intelligence has planned and wrought, we are walking where God has been before us, and still is. If we study nature with reverence, seeking God in all that his hand has made, we cannot fail to become wiser and better, more loving, more adoring, more devout.

*

"True education consists more in a power to master a subject,— to perceive, discover, and marshal facts in relation thereto, than in the mere accumulation of those facts." The little purse of Fortunatus, in the fairy tale, which never contained more than one piece of gold at a time, but in which the one piece was always found when the owner sought for it, was better to him than a storehouse filled full of the precious coins. — *School Report*, 1880.

THE TEACHER AND HER WORK.

The true and earnest teacher carries her pupils with her in school and out; she studies them as individuals, and as classes. She studies for means to influence them, and to lead them to influence each other to a good end. She seeks to inform herself of all those things that may benefit her pupils, which may interest them in the pursuit of knowledge and truth. She studies how she may best arouse the sluggish, and direct the energies of the quick and active. Her own faculties are in full activity; she imparts, as the forces of nature are imparted, by presence and contact with her pupils, an enthusiasm for learning, a hunger and thirst for knowledge. She outgrows all methods that she has learned, and communicates her ideas and draws out her pupils' powers she knows not how. They learn by simple contact with her enkindled nature, they know not how. She teaches "with brains," and her pupils work with their brains, desiring to know, and rejoicing in the consciousness of an awakened intellect.

Working herself from the standpoint of high moral and religious principles, she leads those whom she teaches to love truth and goodness, and to aspire for themselves to the highest good. To be a good teacher is to be one of the noblest of the workers with God. But what shall we say of some of the aspirants to this office who are so little in advance of those whom they wish to teach that the preparatory examination is a terror, and who, when that is passed, and they established at the head of a school, feel that the goal of life has been attained, and congratulate themselves that they no longer are obliged to go to school and learn lessons! And what of those who will avow that they desire to become teachers because they do not wish to "work" for a living! — *School Report, Littleton*, 1879.

Teachers are a hard-working class. They do the best they know for their pupils. Some teachers labor also to improve themselves; the best all do this, and the more success and experience a teacher has gained, the more earnest we find her in the work of self-improvement. But there are teachers who make less effort for this than would a skilful mechanic who seeks to keep himself in a high rank. He does not consider his trade learned when his apprenticeship ends. If he has a "nice job" he plans it carefully, sharpens his tools, having selected with care those best adapted to his purpose. But we may find a young teacher who leaves her studies as she takes her place at "*the* desk." She reads no educational journal, forms no associations with other teachers, visits no schools. She hears the pupils recite from the book, having nothing to add by which their interest may be aroused and a desire for knowledge awakened. Then she wonders why the children dislike school, why they are so dull, restless, and disobedient. No teacher can be expected to know everything at every moment, but an earnest teacher can, and should, know the lessons to be taught each day in her school. She can, like Napoleon in his battles, be always strong at the point of attack. She can keep her own mind bright and active and capable of imparting brightness and activity to the minds made to come in contact with her own, by reading and study and observation, outside the branches she is teaching. The teacher's first duty is with herself. She is the instrument by which her pupils are to be benefited, — the chronometer by which the ship is to be sailed. — *School Report, Littleton*, 1880.

In view of the responsibilities of the hard-working and much-enduring class of teachers, it sometimes seems strange that any one should be found who would dare to undertake to keep a school. One term at school has often been the turning point in the life of a child. In it he has gained an impulse which has set his face towards a resolute and honest manhood, or, failing that, his downward tendencies have been confirmed or new ones acquired, so that his life failure is sure. The best teachers are not always those who have the greatest confidence in their finished preparation for their work. Teaching is not a trade, or a trick, to be once learned and then practised without further thought: the oldest and best teacher is often the one who most feels her deficiencies and who labors most earnestly to remedy them. The most successful teachers are those who can awaken and set in action the powers of the child's mind so that he may love learning and delight to work out for himself the difficulties of his lesson. There may be capabilities with little outward sign, and we know not what may be within the dullest exterior. Some teachers kill the germs of progress in a child's mind by a want of respect for his ability and sympathy with his efforts to improve. And the ambition of the child is sometimes crushed by a want of personal respect which some teachers exhibit towards their scholars. One of the noblest utterances of the lamented Gov. Andrew was, " I never knew what it was to turn away from a man because he was low, or to despise one because he was weak." Like calls out like; if a teacher respects her pupils as individuals, as fellow human beings, the cases are few that she will not be respected in return. And further still, the moral character of the child should be trusted until the fullest evidence of guilt has been found. The pupils of Dr. Arnold used to say, " It's a shame to lie to the Doctor, for he always believes what we say to him."

Many well-meaning teachers fail in

creating an interest in the subjects taught because they begin at the wrong end. They teach the alphabet and numbers, and to name places on the map of the earth's surface. But let them first secure a respect for learning, respect for a book as containing mysteries desirable to be unfolded, let the pupils have a glimpse of the wonders of mathematical knowledge, to an understanding of which the daily lessons are steps, let them contemplate the earth rolling in space, with its continents and seas, before they are required to commit to memory the names of cities and towns, and an interest may be excited which may make the lessons in school as interesting as those learned in a menagerie. The word-method of teaching reading has taken the place of the old way of beginning with the letters. Let the principle involved here be applied to other things. No one would require an infant to learn the names of the legs, arms, back, seat, and rounds of a chair, before he had seen or could name the chair itself, yet children are every day learning facts, dates, tables, and rules without the least comprehension of the wholes of which these form a part.

And going still further back, before attempting to teach anything, the teacher should seek to gain the confidence of her pupils and the power to control not their bodies only, not their thoughts only, but the desires and emotions of their hearts, that she may lead them to love goodness and truth, to be honest and honorable, to live with clear consciences so that all truth, physical or moral, may be clearly seen and pursued with untrammelled energies. The intellect is often aroused through the heart, and the desire for learning and the love for it may be enkindled by one who imparts but little actual instruction. It is in the exciting of interest that the teacher's province really exists. Many of the great men of the world were dull boys, and many of our most useful men of to-day can give the date of their awakened faculties. Then let the teacher study her pupils, search for the avenues to their minds, see what will interest them — it is better sometimes for them to be interested in mischief or play, than wholly dull; if they can be alive to one thing they may be to another, and activity once awakened may be directed and controlled. In all things let her remember that all instruction, all incentive to action, must have in view the development of the highest in the child's nature — the moral part; that a noble character is the end and aim of all true human effort; that the intellect is to be stimulated in order that it may be used in the service of God and Humanity. — *School Report, Littleton*, 1881.

FROM LETTERS OF TRAVEL.

Near Drachenfels on the Rhine, 1859. "We heard on our arrival that we were in the same hotel that had been honored a few months before by the young Prince of Wales and his party, and I fancied for awhile that they thought their former guest had sent his mother to make them a visit. Such running to and fro, and such tumbling of people one over another, I never saw. We were shown to a room at last as large as a Boston church, with one single bed in each corner, and a few other articles of furniture ranged up and down the sides."

Friburg, 1859. "We went at twilight to hear the organ. It was one of the grandest addresses to the ear I ever heard. We had long been *seeing* great things, and now our ears were to take their sum. The imitation of the human voice is very wonderful. It is weird-like, affecting you with a kind of superstitious awe, as if you were in the presence of a naked soul striving for utterance and wandering to find its home. A voice without a body! The performer closed with 'The Village Festival,' in which a thunder-storm was imitated. The whole force of the organ is here exhibited, and as the thunder reverberated through the vaulted roof of the old cathedral, it seemed in the darkness as if some Prospero had enticed you into his cave and had called up a real tempest to overwhelm you."

Rome, 1859. "St. Peter's is the noblest building on earth, and I do not believe it is in the power of man ever to excel it. Inside and outside, above and below, everywhere, it is grand and imposing.

"Did I tell you about meeting the Pope? We were driving through one of the arches between St. Peter's and the

Vatican, and met him in a narrow place, with just room to pass. Our driver and courier got out and knelt down: we bowed a little to him and received a very gracious bow in return.

"I have seen one grand popish ceremony and procession. We went early to the church of San Carlo where the Pope was to attend mass. We waited an hour or two while the church was filling with people of every class and with several detachments of soldiers. You must remember that some churches here would contain ten or fifteen like ours at home, roof, steeple and all, and still not be full. These soldiers, all in their best uniforms, were ranged up and down on each side where his Holiness was to pass, and stationed all about in the church. I was so simple as to imagine that the Pope was to walk from his door to his seat prepared under a canopy near the high altar; but it seems from the time he becomes Pope he is never seen to walk except the step or two he is obliged to take beside the altar. I cannot tell you of all the appendages, but at length he came in a high chair, resting on poles covered with red velvet, and borne on the shoulders of four men. The people all knelt as he passed them in the church. We held our heads down a little, — peeping up all the time not to lose any part of the sight.

"He was carried to his seat, his robes arranged and his cap adjusted by the cardinals in attendance. Then there was a long ceremony of going up, kneeling and kissing the Pope's hand (covered by his robe), by the cardinals and priests. Then followed the mass, during which we left for the American Consul's house which was near, and from the balcony of which we had a fine view of the procession."

*

Vienna, Jan. 8, 1860. "We have met with no accident or trouble more serious than that from the porters over our baggage at the various stopping places. When you are leaving a place or arrive at one, these porters, *facchini* they call them, will make a rush at your trunks, and every one who can manage to put a finger on one will come for you and demand a franc, about twenty cents. One set of men will carry the trunks where you *don't* want them, and then you must pay another set to take them where you do. All travellers are subject to this annoyance."

*

Dresden, Feb. 14, 1860. "Everything is genuine German here. At dinner all stand silent for a moment before sitting down, while the master of the house bows to the company, wishing them good appetite, after which all sit down and help each other or themselves in a very simple fashion. The lady of the house rises to dismiss the table, while all shake hands and wish *gesegnete mahlzeit,* or, 'May your meal be blessed to you.'

"We have here the genuine German feather bed to sleep under. We thought we had seen it before at hotels, where we often had a sort of large cushion covering about half the bed at the foot, and sometimes a down quilt; but here we have the genuine, under which we sleep and nothing else. It is quite large, very light, of the softest down, covered with linen like a pillow, which covering is changed as sheets would be. We crawl under this and sleep well. It seems to have no weight, and fits down close to you and is as comfortable as possible. We laughed so much at first that we could hardly go to bed. You feel as if you were in the bottom of a big squash pie!

"You will be amused to see the idea the people here have of the Sabbath. It was the same in Italy. Here in the churches they appear very devout, and as far as I can make it out the preaching is well enough. The hymns I can read, and they are very devotional. The family where we are, go occasionally to the church in the morning, have about noon the best dinner of the week, then usually go to walk and take coffee and cakes at some one of the numerous cafés to be found in the direction of all the walks. When they come home, if they are disposed, they take their embroidery or other work, perhaps go in the evening to a theatre or a ball. I cannot understand it. They believe the Bible, and have a great deal of reverence for sacred things. The shops are all closed on Sundays except the cafés, cook shops, and provision stores, but they have no idea of keeping the day as we do."

*

Chihuahua, Mexico, March 21, 1886.
"I never realized what a country would

be without grass. It is as naked as the road everywhere, except the little cultivated bits. The mountains look like heaps of stuff thrown out from a furnace; no trees and no grass or bushes upon them.

"The people interest me most of anything. We were taken in carriages and omnibuses to the city, a mile or two away, this morning, and to a long ride all around the city. We went to the Catholic service in the Cathedral and heard a very vigorous sermon, which I hope did the numerous hearers much good. I understood only one word.

"The people, very old and very young, infants of all qualities and conditions, knelt on the bare stone or board floors. There were old, shrivelled, and dirty, ragged Indian men and women, Spanish women and girls with the shawl over the head, some with cotton gowns, muslin, gingham, and calico, and some with fine silks. One wore a delicate lilac brocade, trimmed with white lace, and a thin black shawl over her head just as you put one on to run out after the chickens. Some young men were like dry goods clerks, quite in

American style, but most of the men had *serapes*, a kind of striped carriage blanket worn rather gracefully over the shoulders. No hats were worn in church, and they take them off when they pass the church door: but the hat generally seems the best part of them, high crowned, broad brimmed, and often trimmed with beads, cords, and tassels. But the Mexican is in his glory when astride any kind of animal, horse, mule, or donkey. He appears a veritable king in his manner, and keeps the beast galloping without cessation. The bright-colored *serape* and other toggery give him a picturesque appearance."

MISCELLANEOUS SELECTIONS.

What is Poetry?—There are two classes of ideas: one connected with the material and the other with the spiritual part of our nature. That which is itself material, and does not in any way connect with the spiritual, is prosaic. That which is spiritual, or connected with what is spiritual, is poetic. So much of religion even as has reference to the performance of certain duties, or to the securing of one's own safety in another world, is prosaic;

that of it, which associates duty with the sentiment of love, is poetic. The every-day duties of life, considered as terminating in physical good, are prose: considered as promotive of spiritual good or proceeding from a sentiment which is elevated, they become poetry. Poetry implies a certain degree of elevation. Ideas may have almost any degree of this, and in proportion as they rise above the common current of any one's thoughts do they become poetic to that person. Hence, what is poetry to one is prose to another: and the everyday thoughts of one are poetry to others. And we talk of a poem for poets, that is, one that is as far above the ordinary range of poetry as that is above common life. Ideas are elevated as they become connected with the spiritual part of our nature. A common act is poetic as emanating from a lofty sentiment. The life of Hiawatha in its events was as prosaic as that of many other Indians; but connecting these events with his mission to his people, they become poetic. The matron in her cottage, cutting a loaf of bread, is prosaic enough, but viewed by a former lover as dispensing food to the children of her love, the scene is full of poetry. An Irishman cutting rocks is not poetic, but when Ajax storms and hurls a mighty rock against his enemies, we think the circumstance not unfit for a place in a poem. The same principle is true applied to natural scenery, and in painting and music. Poetry, then, comprises those ideas which are elevated above the ordinary range.

Woman and Temperance Work. — Our temperance orators must always fall back on the moral and religious forces necessary to make the laws effective. And who so well adapted to exert the influence needed as women? They can speak their minds without being suspected of self-seeking motives behind the spoken words. What they say and do is for the truth and right, independent of selfish ends. Women are said to be, and I believe are, as a rule, more spiritually minded, more elevated in life and aim, than men, and more fitted to uplift and inspire the downfallen and the weak. Their influence in the temperance work is acknowledged as the purest and most ennobling the world has known.

Women can and should supply motives, encourage and stimulate men to pure and noble aims in the often demoralizing and depressing influences of their environment. [1890.]

Woman and Man. — In answer to the question, "If woman has not the manly form of Webster, how can she have his gigantic mind?" I have yet to learn if, even in material things, size is a criterion of value or of power. Is not a dollar's worth of gold as valuable as a dollar's worth of feathers? Is not a ball from the cannon's mouth more effective than the vast weight of Ajax's rock? and a steam engine than the ponderous battering ram of ancient times? While we wonder at the massive Sphinx, we admire the Apollo. The pyramids are vast, but even in their completeness they fail to call forth the emotion which the ruins of Palmyra's Temple of the Sun, or the Parthenon, commands. Then, among both animals and men, size is never the standard of power. The lion is the king of beasts, a much smaller animal than the ox, but how much more terrible. The powers of woman, while not equal, *i. e.*, alike in all respects, may be equivalent to those of man. A circle may contain as much surface as a square, but will you say the square is larger because its diagonal is greater than the diameter of the circle? The temperaments of man and woman are dissimilar. Hence, the manifestations of mind, when of the same character, will be unlike. A woman may sing bass, but it will not be a man's bass: so a man may sing treble, and none of us in listening to it will doubt the propriety of the name "falsetto" when applied to the performance. The man and the woman may sing the same part, and while his excels in strength and power, hers is an octave higher. Anatomists tell us that the female brain is distinctive from that of man, that it is lighter, and that this difference is discernible even in infancy. The mind, therefore, is not dependent on a large amount of matter for its manifestations, inasmuch as we are all accustomed to regard angels and disembodied spirits as enjoying an advantage over us, and we speak always intelligibly of the " fetters of the flesh."

Books. — Many hours you will spend in the companionship of books, those potent solaces of human grief, and sources of treasures of knowledge. Through them you may go back in your sympathies to the inhabitants of Troy among her smoking ruins; your hearts may swell with Cæsar as he passes the Rubicon; you may contend with Luther against the storms of opposition of the "Man of Sin" in his anger; your hearts may sigh with Bonaparte as he sees his last hope cut off on the field of Waterloo; or you may weep with our own Washington as he bids adieu to his companions in arms at the close of a nation's struggle. But books are at best silent teachers, and we know how much better a subject may be comprehended and impressed on the memory when associated with the tones and looks of a living teacher. Though many have made progress alone and unassisted, we cannot estimate the amount of labor thus expended which might have been better employed, nor can we know how much greater would have been the attainments under suitable directors.

Mental Growth. — The happiness of childhood is often overrated. We could not, with our present knowledge, enjoy the amusements of another childhood, even if free from care. The only pure and perfect happiness arises from a conscientious discharge of duty to God and man, of which a child knows little. As we progress in mental and moral knowledge our sources of happiness are multiplied. If, in the course of our existence here, where the aspirations of the soul are constantly retarded by the body, we can perceive the progress of the mental faculties, how much more rapid must be this advance in that state in which the imprisoned soul shall be set free and pursue its education under the immediate tuition of an Omniscient Teacher. If we can trace our increased capacity for enjoyment in this imperfect state, how will all our powers be expanded and filled with unalloyed bliss in that world where the disembodied spirit shall rest in the bosom of the Giver of all happiness.

The mind is not constituted with the desire and capacity for improvement without objects to gratify its longings. When ages on ages have rolled away, every moment of which has been spent in the accumulation of new truths, we shall have but just begun to learn. Eternity will exhibit no point beyond which there is naught to discover. The nature of the mind is such, that were there such a point, all beyond must be misery. Nothing more to learn! An angel in the abodes of bliss would shed more bitter tears than angel ever dropped before, if God could show him no further proofs of skill and goodness. The mind is fitted to progress, without limit, in knowledge of the countless perfections of Him who purchased our salvation. With the moral as with the intellectual faculties, increase of cultivation enlarges the capacity.

Genius and Toil. — It is one of the brightest tokens of true genius to be able to surmount difficulty after difficulty. Genius carries no enchanter's wand with which to level hills and mountains, but she brings to her task implements of hard and persevering toil, and with the labor of her own unwearied hand she completes her everlasting monument. And upon whom her mantle of inspiration has truly fallen, effort, the most laborious, will not be scorned. There are those who, professing her power, have shone forth like the coruscations of some flashing meteor, to dazzle but not illume, who, blinded by their own unsteady light, have stumbled over the difficulties in their onward path. But those whom she most highly favors, shining as the meridian sun, perceive obstructions but to overcome them. Hours of tedious study, by the solitary lamp in the silent watches of the night, must be spent by him who would go forth in the kindly light of day and astonish the world by his achievements. It gives nothing to man without great labor. Deprive him of money, alienate his friends, leave him destitute of every external aid, you place no insuperable barrier before him. The way is plain which leads up to the bright temple of happiness and honor, and he will reach it, for

"Under the whole heaven there is nothing difficult. It is only that men's minds are not determined."

The Power of Thought. — By means of thought, the penman of Holy Writ, with supernatural power, holds up to the straining vision of the poor earth worm, not the mirage of fancy, but promises of future glory surpassing the conceptions of the most vivid imagination; promises on which the soul may rest as the infant in the arms of its mother, and, pillowed upon them, may fall asleep and awake to realize their eternal stability. Thought is the connecting chain between man and the Deity. He may twist together its fibres and enlarge its links, till, by it, he can almost climb from earth to heaven. [1844.]

Life and Poetry. — Life without poetry is dark and unlovely. It is but the skeleton of an existence, without flesh or drapery. Even if the poet's dream, like a half transparent veil, hide the deformities of the world, and I am ever deceived, — tear not the veil away; still let me dream of beauty, of love, of happiness.

Mistakes. — There is perhaps nothing with which we are more impatient than mistakes, either our own or those of other people. If a bad thing is deliberately planned and carried out to the end, we may have some degree of satisfaction in success, we may take some pleasure in seeing the means adapted to the end and the inevitable workings of cause and effect: but mistakes seem all wrong, nobody planned for them, they are indeed in opposition to everybody's plan, and often a surprise and discomfiture to everybody. They are often mortifying to our self-esteem: we condemn our folly in not having foreseen our way better, and perhaps complain of Providence in not having made us wiser or more capable. There are fatal mistakes, mistakes that can never be remedied in this life, which may affect our happiness for eternity. But many of these disagreeable experiences are the necessary discipline of a good life, and must be accepted as a part of the machinery of our existence by which we are enabled to climb to higher and better things.

A story is told of Napoleon which illustrates this. He once found himself with several of his officers by the seaside, at nightfall, with the tide coming in. They all became bewildered and lost entirely all notion of their right direction. The waters were about them and they knew not where to look for the shore. At length the hero of Austerlitz and Marengo called to his companions, ordering a halt. He then commissioned the several individuals to set out, each in a different direction, while he stood still to hear their reports. A few moments sufficed to show them in which direction was the deep sea and in which was the shallow water of the shore. Now, every one who exerted himself in this search was an agent in its success. Those who went in the wrong direction contributed, not less than the one who was sent towards the land, to its discovery. So our numerous mistakes may be a necessary antecedent to our ultimate success. Provoking as they sometimes are, they teach us what is not the right direction, and train us to watchfulness and caution for the future. We do not forget a lesson thus learned. According to the homely adage, "Bought wit is better than taught wit, if you don't buy it too dear."

Social Intercourse.—We have all experienced the enjoyment of social intercourse. We have felt our heart leap with delight as we have clasped the hand of some tried friend, and have drank in new life as we have exchanged thoughts and feelings and opened our souls each to each in loving sympathy. We know the pleasure there is in the social hour, when two or many meet, desiring each to say and to do those things which may entertain or amuse one another. Such enjoyment does us good. It is good to be free from care and worry, if for only an hour; to feel that life is a blessed and beautiful thing, and that God is to be thanked for its gift. It is good to renew our interest in our fellow mortals and to increase our knowledge of them. Then the intellect is stimulated by contact with other intellect, by the sport of the light tournament as truly as by the tug and roar of the heavy artillery. And persons learn, as they meet, to set a right value on their own powers; the conceited lose some of their too abundant plumes: while the timid gain courage and strength by contact with those who overawed them at a distance. Every one sees the power of the well-bred, unselfish behavior and cultivated manners and language which society promotes, to influence men and women for good or for evil. And yet the time and attention required by society are either grudgingly bestowed or refused altogether! This may be, perhaps, because we undervalue the opportunities we have for social intercourse. We feel ourselves, possibly, superior to those we meet on ordinary occasions. If the company which we are invited to enter be composed of distinguished persons, very well, — but these *common* people! We forget that our superiors, whom we enjoy so much, must find us the *common* people, such as we despise, and that the occasion so dull to us, may be, to some humble soul, a rare opportunity.

We do not always appreciate the attractions which "society" possesses for most young people. The power of a church to keep the young within its influence often turns upon its character in a social point of view. Young people *must* have society, and if it is not found in one church it is in another, or even where no influence of church or Christian people is exerted. In the plan of extending the kingdom of God through a visible church, the social element in man's nature was intended to play an important part, and in connection with the church, man's social nature should be cultivated. And notice some things which refined and refining social intercourse is, and is not. First, it is *intercourse;* it is not sitting or standing around in groups, gazing at one another or into vacancy, with no conversation. In the second place, it is respectful and dignified; it is not a promiscuous rushing together of people young and old, with the single idea of freedom and frolic. Thirdly, it should be general; people who wish to see and to converse with only one individual should not enter the social circle to do so. And, finally, there should be real conversation, not mere chit-chat, or giggling nonsense, but each one in going into society should fix upon some topics of interest in his own mind, on which he may seek or impart information; he may propose some question which may be lightly discussed, and by which mental activity may be excited; or he may, by puzzle, anecdote, or game, amuse or entertain some who would otherwise help to form the not enviable bouquet of wall-flowers. — *From the "Colby Voice,"* 1872.

Culture and Religion. — High mental cultivation failed to teach the Athenians anything of the true God or of acceptable worship to him. They furnish a melancholy illustration of the necessity of a revelation of the will of God towards the race of fallen man. The wisest philosopher of Athens failed to satisfy himself as to the nature and attributes of God, or to form a system of ethics unobjectionable to himself. One precept of the heaven-taught Jesus of Nazareth has done more to exalt, purify, and bless the human family than all the philosophy of antiquity. [1853.]

Thoughts on Death. — I like to contemplate death in the manner Bishop Butler views it, as analogous to birth; that it is only a change of form; that like birth it brings us into a higher and more perfect state of existence. May we not regard the change as an entrance into a state of freedom, one in which all the powers of the soul will be infinitely expanded, better able to take in lofty and noble ideas, better able to study the truths with which the universe abounds. One reason, perhaps, why the thought of death is so unwelcome is our want of spirituality. We forget that we have a soul as well as a body, in the plenitude of our care for the latter, and the thought fixes itself more upon the situation of the body than the state of the soul. We think of the coffin and the winding sheet, of the cold, lonely grave, of the decay of the body, instead of the released soul rejoicing in heavenly bliss. We forget to look beyond the grave, forget that " legions of angels cannot confine the spirit there," but that, if blessed with the Christian's hope, it is rejoicing in the bosom of its Saviour.

It is a beautiful idea of Swedenborg that we may, even before death, become sensible of spiritual presence ; that we may hold converse with departed spirits ; that there is a spiritual medium of interchange of thought which all those who live aright may attain to. However fanciful this may be, we cannot doubt that the spirit is susceptible of a higher development, and that we need not be so fettered by the flesh as we are at present. We may so live that pale death may come to us in far other aspect than one of terror. [1845.]

Suffering and Sorrow. — In our present state, sympathy with the sorrows of others does not make us wholly miserable: it may even be more ennobling, and consequently more productive of happiness, than indifference to such sorrows. I saw at a depot one summer, a woman evidently near the last stage of consumption, with one or two friends about to set out on a journey. They were all in humble circumstances, but neat and respectable. It was painful to look on the woman, as her neighbors and friends ran in to take their leave of her, previous to what they seemed to feel was their final separation, and her attendants with tearful eyes ministered to her wants. I was quite overcome. Misery, I thought, — the world is full of misery. But dwelling on the scene I thought how much better that these poor women should gather about their friend and weep with her and for her, than that they should be insensible to grief, and I questioned whether they were not both better and happier for this exercise of tender emotion. And it seemed to me that there was no evil, after all, but from which good might be educed.

❧

Our capacity for loving will be infinitely increased in eternity. It cannot be that those whom we once loved, to whom our hearts were knit by all but the highest spiritual sympathy, can there find no place in our affections.

❧

Fadeless Beauty. — It is the influence of the soul moulding the gross clay to its will that gives the highest beauty, even to a mortal countenance. Who has not learned to look beneath the fair exterior for this gem which burns with living radiance far above that of senseless matter? And when, on the morning of the resurrection, the redeemed of the Lord shall come up, when the power of perceiving spiritual existence shall have been infinitely increased, how then shall the beauty of a pure and holy spirit strike upon that assembled multitude! Then shall the saints shine in unfading loveliness, and the beauty of holiness fill every soul. [1844.]

TO HANNAH P. DODGE.

O FRIEND and teacher! Thy good message true
Has rung both clear and strong among the oft
Uncertain sounds, which, vaguely sweet and soft,
So lulled our consciences that they could view
As beautiful some error robed anew:
But when thy clarion note rung out aloft,
Our souls marched on in triumph, as they doffed
All cumbrous sophistries, to walk with you.
Speed on thy message, that forevermore
It may awaken silent souls to speech,
And through its invitation nerve to reach
Those heights remote, which barriers seemed
    before.
Activities of life there are, which wear
Away the earth, to show the soul more fair.

HELEN V. CLOUES.

www.ingramcontent.com/pod-product-compliance
Lightning Source LLC
Chambersburg PA
CBHW020906230426
43666CB00008B/1339